Rambling on the Rocks

Walking Northern Ireland's Natural Landscape

K. Lemon, M. Cooper and A. Donald

D1322369

Department for the
Economy
www.economy-ni.gov.uk

GSNI
Geological
Survey of
Northern
Ireland
www.bgs.ac.uk/gsni

Thanks are due to the following organisations for providing images and for assistance on walking routes: Belfast Hills Partnership, Causeway Coast & Glens Heritage Trust, Colin Glen Trust, Marble Arch Caves Unesco Global Geopark, Mourne Cooley Gullion Geotourism Project, Mourne Heritage Trust, Northern Ireland Environment Agency, Ring of Gullion AONB, Ring of Gullion Landscape Partnership and the Sperrins Gateway Landscape Partnership.

All photographs are © Crown Copyright expect for those listed below:
Front and back cover © Alistair Hamill.
Pages iv, 30, 38, 47, 88, 98 © Chris Hill
Pages 2, 62, 63, 64, 66, 68, 70, 72, 74, 75 © Marble Arch Caves Unesco Global Geopark
Pages 10, 11, 48, 49, 50, 52, 53, 60, 61 © Alex Donald
Pages 12, 21, 22, 28, 34, 35, 42, 54, 78, 82, 86 © Esler Crawford
Page 14 © Josemaria Toscano | Dreamstime.com
Page 18 © Colin Glen Trust
Pages 24, 44, 46, 85, 86 © Kirstin Lemon
Page 26 © Monicaminciu | Dreamstime.com
Page 84 © Causeway Coast and Glens Heritage Trust
Page 32 © Patrick McElwee Photography | Dreamstime.com
Page 33 © Oisin Patenall, Creative Commons BY-SA 2.0
Pages 36, 39, 40, 43, 99 © Ring of Gullion AONB
Pages 92, 94, 95 © Sperrins Gateway Landscape Partnership

Excerpt from 'Eureka Street' from Eureka Street by Robert McLiam Wilson 1996. Reproduced with kind permission from Arcade Publishing.
Excerpt from 'The Glens' from Collected Poems by John Hewitt 1997. Reproduced with kind permission by Blackstaff Press Ltd.
Excerpt from 'Shancoduff' from Collected Poems by Patrick Kavanagh. Copyright © Patrick Kavanagh 1958, 1959, 1960, 1962, 1963, 1964, 1965, 1966. Copyright © The Trustees of the Estate of the late Katherine B. Kavanagh, through the Jonathan Williams Literary Agency.
Excerpt from 'The Lion the Witch and the Wardrobe' by CS Lewis. Copyright © CS Lewis Pte Ltd 1950.
Excerpt from 'Decommissioned' by Seamus O' hUltacháin 1997. Reproduced with kind permission from Seamus O' hUltacháin.
Excerpt from 'Inheritance' by Mark Cooper. Reproduced with kind permission from Mark Cooper.
Excerpt from 'The Sperrins' from Where the Three Rivers Meet by Aine MacAodha 2008. Reproduced with kind permission from Aine MacAodha.

This publication contains aerial photography and topographic mapping that is Crown Copyright and is reproduced with the permission of Land & Property Services under Delegated Authority from the Controller of Her Majesty's Stationery Office, © Crown Copyright and database right 2017. Permit Number: 170052.

Contours, coastline and lakes are derived from data published on opendatani.gov.uk under the Open Government Licence: nationalarchives.gov.uk/doc/open-government-licence/version/3/

Printed by W & G Baird.
Bibliographical reference: 2017. Lemon, K., Cooper, M. and Donald, A. Rambling on the Rocks: Walking Northern Ireland's Natural Landscape. Geological Survey of Northern Ireland, Belfast.

First published 2017
ISBN 978-0-85272-870-3
© Crown Copyright 2017

Contents

Introduction

"In every walk with Nature one receives far more that he seeks"
— John Muir, founder of the National Parks

The landscapes of Northern Ireland reflect close to 650 million years of the Earth's history. During that time, the country has undergone many dramatic changes including being covered by shallow tropical seas, experiencing searing hot desert conditions, being ravaged by icy wastelands, and witnessing fiery volcanic eruptions.

This long and complex history, coupled with its current temperate climate and location as an island on the edge of the Atlantic ocean, has led to Northern Ireland being home to some of the most diverse landscapes found anywhere on Earth.

Over the millennia, the dramatic beauty of the landscapes has inspired a multitude of world-famous artists, poets and writers. Rarely however has the question been raised as to how these unique landscapes formed, or about what they can tell us of Northern Ireland's capricious past.

The landscapes of Northern Ireland have also influenced the rich natural and cultural heritage for which this part of the world is famous. The wealth of achaeological and historical sites, myths and legends, and the extensive range of plants and wildlife are all a result of the vast diversity of geology found beneath our feet.

One of the best ways to discover and understand Northern Ireland's rich tapestry of landscapes is to explore them on foot. Using this guide you will be able to uncover and appreciate some of the 650 million year history for yourself.

The walks have been arranged by county and cover all of the major landscapes including well-known places such as the Mourne Mountains and the Causeway Coast. Some of the walks are off the beaten track but are no less impressive. Why not take a bit of time out and discover something new about the landscapes of Northern Ireland?

Using this guide

Walking is a wonderful way to explore the natural landscapes of Northern Ireland and by following this guide you will experience some of the best on offer. In order to get the most out of each walk it is suggested that you read the following information before you embark on any of the routes.

Walks have been graded and classified as easy, leisurely, moderate and strenuous and full details of these classifications can be found below. Many of the walks follow existing waymarked routes, and if this is the case will have a limited amount of directional information provided. Where there are no waymarkers, detailed directions are given. In all cases, a basic map of the route, including key points along the way are included.

There is a huge variety of walks for you to enjoy, ranging from short circular to longer linear routes. To help you decide which will suit you best, a table with essential information has been provided (page 5).

Time: A guide to the length of time the walk should take. This is based on average walking pace so actual times may vary.

Distance: Given in both kilometres and miles.

Grade: Walks are graded for difficulty as outlined below:

Easy: Walks for anyone who does not have a mobility difficulty, a specific health problem or considers themselves unfit. Suitable for pushchairs if they can be lifted over occasional obstructions. Comfortable shoes or trainers can be worn.

Leisurely: Walks for reasonably fit people with at least a little country walking experience. May include unsurfaced rural paths. Walking boots and warm, waterproof clothing are recommended.

Moderate: Walks for people with country walking experience and a good level of fitness. May include some steep paths and open country. Walking boots and warm, waterproof clothing are essential.

Strenuous: Walks for experienced country walkers with an above average fitness level. May include hills and rough country. Walking boots and warm, waterproof clothing are essential.

Is it for me? This provides an indication as to who or what the walk is suitable for, whether this is for adults, children, pushchairs or dog walkers (with dogs on leads), or a combination of all of these.

Start / parking: The location of the start point as well as the nearest car parking area, if these are not the same.

Nearest town: The nearest town is given in order to provide a reference point for those not familiar with the areas mentioned.

Refreshments: Should you wish to stock up before you go, or else grab a few supplies afterwards, information on the nearest place to get refreshments has been provided.

Public toilets: The location of the nearest public toilets has also been given.

Public transport: Where public transport can be used details have been provided. It should be noted that not all public transport will take you to the start location of a walk. Where it does not, public transport will leave you a maximum of 5km (3 miles) from the start. In these cases, this has been identified and you may choose to walk the additional distance or arrange alternative transport to the start location. For detailed information please see **translink.co.uk**.

Maps: Relevant map/s are provided for each walk. Whilst we have included a basic map for you, should you wish to have more information on the surrounding area, we recommend that you obtain the appropriate Ordnance Survey map/s listed. This is particularly important for walks categorised as Moderate or Strenuous or in unfamiliar locations. For more detailed geological information the relevant geological maps have been listed and may be purchased from the Geological Survey of Northern Ireland.

Finally, please be aware that should you choose to undertake any of the walks in this guide, regardless of the length and duration, you should bring with you some warm, waterproof clothing, a drink, a snack and always wear stout footwear. Always leave details of where you are going and when you should be back and ideally do not go alone. It must also be emphasised that those walking the routes in this guide do so entirely at their own risk and that neither the Geological Survey of Northern Ireland, nor landowners can be held responsible for any accidents that could occur.

County		Walk	Type	Distance	Time	Grade	Suitable for
Belfast City		Cave Hill	Circular	7km (4.5 miles)	3hrs	Moderate	
		Colin Glen	Circular	6.5km (4 miles)	3hrs	Easy	
Co. Antrim		Runkerry	Circular	8.5km (5.5 miles)	3hrs	Moderate	
		The White Rocks	Linear	6.5km (4 miles)	3 hrs	Easy	
		Slemish	Linear	3km (2 miles)	1–2hrs	Strenuous	
Co. Armagh		Mullaghbane	Circular	13km (8 miles)	4–5hrs	Leisurely	
		Slieve Gullion	Circular	13km (8 miles)	5–6hrs	Strenuous	
		Maghery	Circular	8km (5 miles)	2hrs	Easy	
Co. Down		Scrabo	Circular	5km (3 miles)	2hrs	Leisurely	
		Slieve Donard	Circular	13km (8 miles)	4–5hrs	Strenuous	
		Kearney Point	Circular	5km (3 miles)	1–2hrs	Moderate	
Co. Fermanagh		Gortmaconnell	Linear	8km (5 miles)	2–3hrs	Leisurely	
		Pollnagollum	Circular	7km (4.5 miles)	2hrs	Easy	
		Rossergole	Circular	4km (2.5 miles)	1hr	Easy	
Co. Londonderry		Crockbrack	Circular	13km (8 miles)	4hrs	Strenuous	
		Binevenagh	Circular	12km (7.5 miles)	3–4hrs	Leisurely	
		Barnes	Circular	11km (7 miles)	3hrs	Leisurely	
Co. Tyrone		Lough Fea	Circular	4km (3 miles)	1–2hrs	Easy	
		Fardross	Circular	7km (4.5 miles)	2–3hrs	Easy	
		Knockmany	Circular	13km (8 miles)	5hrs	Leisurely	

☐ Easy

▨ Leisurely

▨ Moderate

▨ Strenuous

 Adults with a good level of fitness

 Adults and families with children (8 years and older)

 Adults and families with children (8 years and older) and dog walkers

 Adults and families with children and dog walkers

 Adults and families with children, including those in pushchairs, and dog walkers

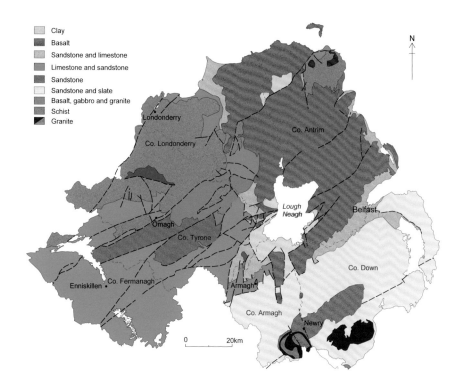

Legend:
- Clay
- Basalt
- Sandstone and limestone
- Limestone and sandstone
- Sandstone
- Sandstone and slate
- Basalt, gabbro and granite
- Schist
- Granite

Londonderry

Co. Londonderry

Co. Antrim

Omagh

Co. Tyrone

Lough Neagh

Belfast

Co. Down

Enniskillen

Co. Fermanagh

Armagh

Co. Armagh

Newry

N

0   20km

Did you know?

Northern Ireland has rocks that represent every major geological time period from 650 million years ago to the present.

Geology Maps

There are two main types of geology map - the one above is known as a bedrock geology map and displays the solid rock (bedrock) only. In Northern Ireland these rocks can be as old as 650 million years. The colours shown on the map correspond with the text on the following pages.

The other main map is known as a superficial geology map and shows the thin layers of sands, gravels, clays and peat that cover the underlying solid rock. These materials accumulated over more recent geological time and are described in The Big Freeze and Warming Up sections that follow.

Rocks & landscapes

The rocks and landscapes of Northern Ireland are diverse and beautiful. The land surface on which we live conceals a long and intricate history of changing climates, sea-levels and a continuing shift in our position on the globe.

650 Million Years

Ancient Foundations

The oldest rocks are thought to have formed as much as 650 million years ago in a period of time known as the Proterozoic and during the early stages of the opening of an ocean called Iapetus. At that time, the continent on which Northern Ireland lay, was close to the South Pole, and was completely separate from the southern half of the island of Ireland. Sediments from this ocean floor now make up large areas of the Sperrin Mountains, north-east Antrim and parts of north-west Fermanagh.

500 Million Years

Vanished Oceans and Mountain Building

Around 500 million years ago, during the Ordovician period, Iapetus started to close and this brought continents into collision resulting in the formation of mountains and chains of volcanic islands. Sediments that had been laid down in the ocean were squeezed up and contorted between the converging continents leading to folding and change referred to as deformation and metamorphism. The metamorphic rocks formed by these processes are called schists. The Sperrins are much eroded stumps of just a small part of the Caledonian Mountain chain that formed at this time. In its entirety, this mountain range would have been as high as the Himalayas.

430 Million Years

Iapetus finally closed about 430 million years ago in the Silurian period. This closure brought the northern and southern parts of the United Kingdom and Ireland together. As the ocean closed sediments were scraped off a slab of ocean crust that was being pushed back into the Earth by a process called subduction. Much of counties Down and Armagh are underlain by a type of sandstone known as greywacke that was formed around this time.

The subduction of ocean crust generated melting within the Earth that lead to the injection, or intrusion, of large bodies of molten rock (magma) into the crust. These bodies, or plutons, cooled and crystallised to form an igneous rock type called granodiorite. The high ground between Slieve Gullion and Slieve Croob in counties Armagh and Down are composed of this rock type.

400 Million Years

Deserts and Tropical Oceans

In the Devonian period, about 400 million years ago, the now joined northern and southern parts of the United Kingdom and the island of Ireland were positioned at the edge of a large continent that lay at desert forming latitudes south of the equator. The Caledonian mountain chain, that had formed during Ordovician and Silurian times was eroding rapidly producing huge volumes of sediment which was transported in valleys by broad, meandering rivers that were subjected to seasonal floods. The rocks that record these events are present in the Clogher Valley of County Tyrone and include red sandstone and conglomerate, which is a rock composed of pebbles and cobbles.

350 Million Years

During early Carboniferous times, about 350 million years ago, the island of Ireland lay near the equator and was covered by shallow seas, teeming with life. Sediments laid down in these seas included lime rich muds and the plentiful remains of creatures such as corals, sea lilies (crinoids), brachiopods and bivalves. The rock that formed from this material is limestone and is found in many parts of County Fermanagh. It is in this limestone that the Marble Arch Caves formed.

In middle Carboniferous times, around 320 million years ago, sea level gradually dropped and the shallow seas were replaced by vast river deltas and thick tropical rainforest. Sand and mud carried by rivers that fed the deltas were deposited and buried to form sandstone and mudstone that now make up many of the upland areas of Fermanagh including Slieve Beagh. Layers of plant material were also preserved at this time and are seen as coal seams in Ballycastle, County Antrim and Coalisland, County Tyrone.

300 Million Years

One World

During the Permian period, from about 300 to 250 million years ago, the Earth's surface was dominated by a supercontinent known as Pangea. The island of Ireland was positioned on the eastern margin of this continent just north of the equator. The early part of the period saw the development of vast regions of arid desert which resulted in the formation of red sandstone and conglomerate. During the later Permian period, about 260 million years ago, sea level began to rise again creating inland seas that gradually shallowed and dried out. Limestone and mudstone exposed at Cultra near Holywood, County Down, are rare examples of rocks that belong to this time period.

250 Million Years

By the Triassic period, 250 to 200 million years ago, the island of Ireland had moved to a position in the northern hemisphere where the Sahara desert now exists. Another episode of arid conditions lead to the formation of giant spreads, or fields, of dunes punctuated by broad rivers that flowed only during seasonal flash floods. The red sandstones that were formed are beautifully exposed in a series of disused quarries around Scrabo Hill, County Down. A gradual return to shallow marine conditions led to the formation of the red mudstone that is present in Colin Glen on the outskirts of Belfast, County Antrim. This mudstone contains thick layers of salt that developed as a consequence of drying out of the seas by evaporation. This salt is now mined in the vicinity of Carrickfergus in County Antrim.

200 Million Years
(Not shown on the simplified map)

The Age of Sea Monsters
Sea level rose again during the Jurassic period, from about 200 to 145 million years ago, and the entire landscape was covered by a shallow sea full of life. Mudstone and limestone from this period have yielded some of the most spectacular fossils found in Northern Ireland and include marine reptiles (dinosaur equivalents) as well as beautifully coiled shells known as ammonites.

145 Million Years
(Not shown on the simplified map)

Warm, clear seas prevailed from about 145 to 65 million years ago during the succeeding Cretaceous period. White limestone, or chalk, that dominates parts of the north and east Antrim Coast were formed at this time. Remarkably chalk is composed almost entirely of microscopic fossils of marine algae called coccoliths. Other larger fossils found within the chalk include sharks teeth, sea urchins, ammonites and the bullet shaped belemnites or devil's thunderbolts.

65 Million Years

Land of Fire
From about 65 million years ago, during the Palaeogene period, Northern Ireland experienced truly explosive conditions and this was due to the opening of the North Atlantic Ocean which led to widespread volcanic activity. Molten rock was spewed from numerous fissures and this spread out over the landscape in the form of lava flows that cooled and crystallised to form a black rock known as basalt. The accumulation of lava flow on lava flow led to the formation of the Antrim Plateau, an area of Northern Ireland most famous for the Giant's Causeway. Molten rock that failed to reach the surface formed plutons of igneous rock such as granite and gabbro that now form striking landscape features such as Slieve Gullion in County Armagh and the Mourne Mountains in County Down.

55 Million Years

25 Million Years

All this volcanic activity was accompanied by earth movements, or faulting, that in some cases lead to the formation of huge depressions, or basins, such as that now occupied by Lough Neagh.

The Big Freeze
The Quaternary period, or the last 2.6 million years, has brought with it a series of ice ages that have had a remarkable impact on the landscape. Although ice only covered the land for relatively short periods of time, the erosion and deposition that occurred has led to some the most distinctive landscape features such as the drumlins around Strangford Lough and the glacial deposits of the Sperrin Mountains.

Warming Up
Since the end of the last ice age, a mere 13,000 years ago, the landscapes of Northern Ireland have continued to change. Natural processes, coupled with the impact of human activities, have led to the development of a number of additional features such as the formation of blanket bog, found in many parts of Northern Ireland.

The city rises and falls like music, like breathing...
Belfast is Rome with more hills: it is Atlantis raised fr[...]
And from anywhere you stand, from anywhere you lo[...]
the streets glitter like jewels, like small strings of sta[...]
However many, whatever size, it is magical.

From 'Eureka Street' by Robert McLiam Wilson

the sea.

Cave Hill and Belfast Castle

Cave Hill

GPS 54.642751, -5.942531 / Irish Grid J 32811 79129

Time: 3 hours
Distance: 7km (4.5 miles)
Grade: Moderate
Type: Circular

Is it for me?
Suitable for adults and families with older children (8 years and over)

Start / Parking
Car parking at Belfast Castle or at Belfast Zoo

Nearest town
Belfast

Refreshments
Belfast Castle

Public Toilets
Belfast Castle

Public Transport
Metro service 1 to Strathmore Park (Belfast Castle) or Bellevue (Belfast Zoo)

Maps
Belfast Discoverer Sheet 15
1:250,000 Northern Ireland Solid Geology

Other Information
Belfast Castle is open daily and admission is free

The iconic cliffs of Cave Hill dominate the Belfast skyline and offer a rare window into the underlying geology of the city. This stunning circular walk provides breathtaking views over Belfast Lough and through the mosaic of natural habitats that make up Cave Hill Country Park.

The walk begins at the interpretation post just before Belfast Castle **(1)** and follows the Cave Hill trail north which is clearly waymarked.

Built by the Donegall family, the castle proudly looks out over Belfast Lough from its vantage point on the slopes of Cave Hill. The current castle was built between 1811 and 1870 and was designed by Charles Lanyon who also designed the Queen's University of Belfast. The stone used in the construction of the building is red sandstone from southern Scotland and is quite different from the surrounding rocks. The area around the castle was originally farmland, but in the 1880s, a major planting exercise transformed it into beautiful woodland, and the castle estate now forms part of the Country Park.

As you follow the Cave Hill trail, you begin to ascend the Cave Hill itself. Located on the edge of the Antrim Plateau, Cave Hill is made up of a dark coloured rock called basalt. Basalt is a type of rock that was once molten and would have formed as lava spewed out over the east of Northern Ireland about 60 million years ago during a period in the Earth's history known as the Palaeogene.

Following the trail north, the path skirts round the edge of the Devil's Punchbowl **(2)**, a name given to a scarp of basalt in the shape of a bowl. From here you will see why this area is called Cave Hill due to the small number of caves found in the hillside. These are man-made caves and are thought to have been early iron mines. There are five in total but from this point you should be able to see at least three of them.

The trail continues to climb and turns south where you will soon see McArt's Fort **(3)**, a former defensive ringfort or rath built on a naturally occurring promontory. The cliff offered protection on one side and on the other a defensive ditch was built. Little remains of the original fort although the ditch is just visible.

Did you know?

The profile of Cave Hill is said to have inspired Jonathan Swift to write Gulliver's Travels as he thought it resembled a sleeping giant.

Keep following the trail that swings west until you reach the summit of Cave Hill, historically known as Ben Madigan. From here there are spectacular views out over the city and Belfast Lough, as well as further afield to the Mourne Mountains, Strangford Lough, Scrabo Tower, the Isle of Man and Scotland on clear days. The summit of Cave Hill is 368 metres above sea level and is clearly visible from all routes north of Belfast. The outline of the rugged basalt cliffs is likened to Napoleon sleeping on the hillside and is often referred to as Napoleon's Nose.

As you look out over Belfast Lough, take time to think about what is happening deep beneath the surface. The north shore of Belfast Lough is home to the only salt mine on the island of Ireland with over half a million tonnes of salt mined here every year. The salt is extracted and used throughout the United Kingdom and Ireland and exported as far afield as the France and USA. The layers of salt formed when this area was covered by a land locked sea some 240 million years ago. As the sea water evaporated, layers of salt were left behind, and over millions of years these layers were buried deep beneath the surface of Belfast Lough.

As you continue west on the trail you will pass through the Ballyaghagan Nature Reserve **(4)**, an area of upland meadow with a rich diversity of wild plants. The path continues downwards and you may catch a glimpse of what lies beneath the dark basalt rocks, when you see white rocks either exposed in the hillside or lying as loose boulders at your feet. This white rock is a type of limestone made up from the shelly remains of countless of microscopic organisms called coccoliths. Coccoliths would have thrived in the warm, shallow waters of an ancient sea that existed

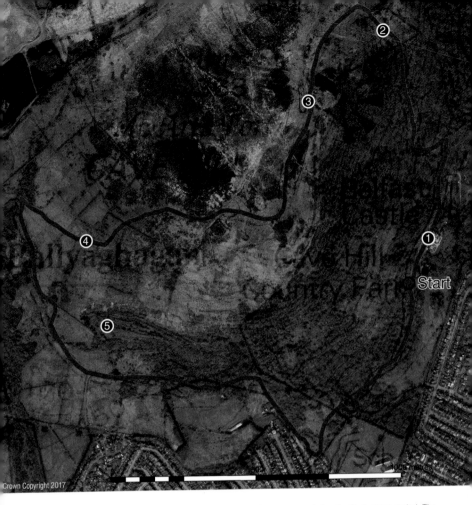

Crown Copyright 2017

Opposite: Built in the 19th century Belfast Castle was designed by Charles Lanyon

here some 80 million years ago during the Cretaceous period. The limestone has since been covered by the basalts that make up the majority of Cave Hill.

White limestone was quarried here during Victorian times and the disused quarry is located just north of the trail **(5)**. The rock was transported to Belfast docks by a horse-drawn railway that ran along what is now known as the Limestone Road. The railway was dismantled in the 1890s.

As you return to the start of the trail, take the time to enjoy the sights, smells and sounds of the woodland that surrounds Belfast Castle.

The Colin River

Colin Glen

GPS 54.56624, -6.014543 / Irish Grid J 28404 70481

Time: 3 hours
Distance: 6.5km (4 miles)
Grade: Easy
Type: Circular

Is it for me?
Suitable for adults, families with children of all ages, and for dog walkers

Start / Parking
Car parking at the Colin Glen Forest Park visitor centre

Nearest town
Belfast

Refreshments
Colin Glen visitor centre

Public Toilets
Colin Glen visitor centre

Public Transport
Metro service 10 stopping at Woodbourne

Maps
Belfast Discoverer Sheet 15
1:250,000 Northern Ireland Solid Geology

Other information
Colin Glen Visitor Centre is open daily. It contains information on the heritage of the area as well as an excellent fossil display.

The Colin Glen Forest Park is a place of tranquillity in an otherwise bustling part of Belfast. The walk follows the course of the Colin River that flows from the nearby Black Mountain into the River Lagan. The glen is managed by the Colin Glen Trust and the National Trust and is a haven for native wildlife. It provides a rare opportunity to see some of the geology that extends under much of the city.

As you leave the car park, go through the pedestrian gate and follow the signs for the Hannahstown Trail (red markers). After a while you will start to climb uphill and depending on what time of year you visit you will see spectacular displays of colour, either from the woodland plants in the spring, or from the turning leaves in the autumn. At the fork in the path, go downhill to the right (still following the red markers).

At the bottom of the hill you will arrive at the Gamekeepers Bridge that you need to cross, but before you do, have a look at the rocks beneath on the right hand side of the river bank (**1**). These dark grey blocky rocks form a dyke, a vertical sheet of igneous rock that cuts through the pre-existing layers of rock that make up the river bed. The dyke formed as molten rock, or magma, was squeezed into a crack in the Earth's surface around 60 million years ago. This magma cooled and hardened to form a rock called dolerite.

As you continue up the path and you will eventually see orange-red rocks on the far bank of the river (**2**). These rocks are mudstones that formed 240 million years ago during the Triassic period, when Northern Ireland lay at similar latitudes to the Sudan in Africa. Despite the desert conditions, inland seas would have existed, many of which were prone to drying out due to intense evaporation. The red mudstones at Colin Glen would have formed on the sea floor of one of these inland seas. You will soon come to the Weir Bridge downstream of which are red mudstones that are mottled with pale green patches (**3**).

Between the Weir Bridge and the next bridge (Tri-Bridge) there is very little bedrock at surface so continue walking until just before the Cantilever Bridge (that takes you under the Glen Road) where you will see some dark grey rocks forming horizontal layers on the opposite bank (**4**). These rocks formed in the Jurassic period around 200 million years ago. Sea-level had begun to rise at

17

Did you know?

Colin Glen was the site of a rare fossil find when a piece of a Jurassic 'sea-monster' called a plesiosaur was found here in 2007.

that time, and the resulting mudstones and limestones contain many fossils such as coiled ammonites, bivalves (sea-shells such as oysters and mussels) and crinoids, as well as pieces of giant marine reptiles such as ichthyosaurus and plesiosaurus.

Continue under the Glen Road and out into the upper Glen where there is a distinct decrease in the quality of the path. Further upstream, the rocks are white limestone **(5)** that would have formed during the Cretaceous period 80 million years ago. The limestone contains many fossils including belemnites (a relative of the squid), sea urchins and even sharks teeth.

Continue north on the path and just before you reach the wooden bridge you may notice a huge crack in the cliff face on the opposite side of the river **(6)**. This is the Colin Glen Fault and is a fracture caused by Earth movements millions of years ago.

At the wooden bridge, turn round and return on the same path until you reach the Tri-Bridge, at which point you should take the path to the right (still following the red markers). As you continue on the path you will start to see the surrounding hillsides of Black Mountain and Divis Mountain that are made of basalt. Look carefully and you will notice horizontal layering in the cliffs. The layers represent different lava flows that buried the landscape some 60 million years ago during the Palaeogene period.

Continue south eastward on the path and you will see, on the right hand side, some spoil heaps and an old clay pit (now used as a fishing lake) **(7)** both of which are evidence of the former brickworks on the site that was active until the 1960s.

own Copyright 2017

Opposite: The Colin River is fed by surface water that flows from the basalt plateau above

Right: Red mudstone exposed in the Colin River just before the Weir Bridge

Return to the car park by following the red markers of the Hannahstown Trail.

Groined by deep glens and walled along the west
by the bare hilltops and the tufted moors,
this rim of arable that ends in foam
has but to drop a leaf or snap a branch
and my hand twitches with the leaping verse
as hazel twig will wrench the straining wrists
for untapped jet that thrusts beneath the sod.

From 'The Glens' by John Hewitt

The Giant's Causeway

Runkerry

GPS: 55.219748, -6.540829 / Irish Grid C 92855 42382

Time: 3 hours
Distance: 8.5km (5.5 miles)
Grade: Moderate
Type: Circular

Is it for me?
Suitable for adults, families with older children (8 years or older)

Start / Parking
Car parking at Beach Road in Portballintrae

Nearest town
Portballintrae

Refreshments
Portballintrae and Giant's Causeway

Public Toilets
Portballintrae and Giant's Causeway

Public Transport
Ulsterbus service 172 runs from Coleraine to Portballintrae

Maps
Coleraine Discoverer Sheet 4, Causeway Coast 1:50,000 Bedrock Geology Sheet 7

Other Information
To ensure safe access to Runkerry Strand, please check tide times before setting out.

The Giant's Causeway Visitor Centre is open daily; admission fees apply.

The Giant's Causeway is undoubtedly Northern Ireland's most famous natural landscape, but most people visit without spending time exploring more of this dramatic coastline. The Runkerry walk gives the chance to see more of this landscape and gives an appreciation of the vast array of features that have helped to gain World Heritage status for this unique area.

The walk begins at the public car park at the end of Beach Road in Portballintrae. Follow the path that leads from the car park towards the beach, cross the Three Quarter Mile Bridge and then bear left to emerge onto Runkerry Beach (also known as Bushfoot Strand).

As you walk, you will see outcrops of black rock; this is basalt and formed as lava spewed out over the north-east of Northern Ireland around 60 million years ago. This volcanic activity was the result of the opening of the North Atlantic Ocean between Europe and North America. The bay is bounded by basalt headlands at either end, with the area in between void of any such outcrop. This is due to the presence of a fault, or a crack in the Earth's surface along which there has been movement. Because of this, white limestone (or chalk) underlies this area which is much less resistant to erosion.

You will notice the sand dunes on your right **(1)**. These are largely inactive and perched on top of glacial till and raised beach deposits. These are obvious at the far end of the beach where glacial material is exposed at the base of the cliff, seen as grey fine-grained material with a variety of cobbles, overlain by beach deposits seen as rounded pebbles and cobbles. The presence of the beach deposit at this height indicates that sea level was much higher in the past.

At the end of the beach **(2)**, bear left on to the path that runs along the front of Runkerry House and follow the cliff path. The path hugs the coastline and offers spectacular views across to Donegal to the far west, as well as towards the Skerries, a small series of islands near Portrush. To the east, on a good day you may be lucky enough to see Scotland.

As you follow the path towards the Giant's Causeway you will appreciate why this area is a World Heritage site, and as you walk you will cross the boundary on to the site. To give it its full title, the

GIANT'S CAUSEWAY AND
CAUSEWAY COAST
WORLD HERITAGE SITE

Did you know?

The greatest find of

Spanish Armada treasure

ever recovered was

from the wrecked ship

the Girona, located

just off the coast of

Portballintrae.

Giant's Causeway and Causeway Coast World Heritage Site was inscribed in 1986 and is one of very few worldwide that have been designated because of geology. The coastline offers a glimpse into the series of events that happened 60 million years ago, when the North Atlantic Ocean was in its infancy.

Continue on the path that will take you past the back of the Causeway Hotel and over the roof of the visitor centre (3). Below you will see more basalt all of which is known as the Lower Basalt Formation, formed in the first phase of widespread volcanic activity. A long hiatus then followed allowing time for intense weathering to affect the top of the basalt, seen in many places in Northern Ireland as the thick orange layer known as the interbasaltic formation. At the same time, a series of rivers eroded valleys into which lava from localised volcanic eruptions flooded. The lava, known as the Causeway Tholeiite Member, ponded in these channels and cooled down evenly, allowing for the formation of the characteristic columns of the Giant's Causeway. Widespread volcanic eruptions resumed sometime later, forming the Upper Basalt Formation which is seen further along the Causeway Coast and completing the sequence of events that contribute to the outstanding universal value of the site.

As you walk down towards the Giant's Causeway, you will pass much of the Lower Basalt Formation before reaching the characteristic columns of the Causeway basalt (4). Continue on the path, looking out for evidence of onion-skin weathering, a typical weathering feature in basaltic rocks, until you reach a series of prominent basalt columns called The Organ. Turn back on yourself and if possible, take the Shepherd's Steps (5) and follow the clifftop path back to the visitor centre, or simply retrace your steps.

Opposite: The boundary stone for the Giant's Causeway and Causeway Coast World Heritage Site

Leave the visitor centre through the car park, emerging onto the road and bear right onto the Runkerry Road before the main junction. Follow this until the next small road to the right (about 250m), and take this road before joining the path by the railway.

Vast numbers of visitors to the Giant's Causeway are not a new phenomenon and many have been flocking to the site since the 18th and 19th centuries. Its popularity can be attributed to a series of watercolour paintings by Irish artist Susannah Drury in the late 18th century that led to it becoming one of the most famous geological localities in the world. The Giant's Causeway Tramway was constructed in the 19th century to transport tourists from Portrush. It closed in 1949 but a new railway was established, opening up part of the route again to the public in 2002.

Continue along the railway path until you see a boardwalk off to right and into the dunes **(6)**, and follow the River Bush until you return to the Three Quarter Mile Bridge and back to the car park.

The White Rocks

The White Rocks

GPS 55.209384, -6.655006 / Irish Grid C 85612 41082

Time: 3 hours
Distance: 6.5km (4 miles)
Grade: Easy
Type: Linear

Is it for me?
Suitable for adults, families with children and dog walkers

Start / Parking
Car parking at Ramore Head Car Park

Nearest town
Portrush

Refreshments
Portrush

Public Toilets
Ramore Head and Dunluce Castle

Public Transport
NI Railways offer services to Portrush via Coleraine from where it is a short walk to the start point

To return to the start of the walk from Dunluce Castle use Ulsterbus Service 132 or from May to September use the Causeway Rambler (Service 402)

Maps
Coleraine Discoverer Sheet 4
Causeway Coast 1:50,000 Bedrock Geology Sheet 7

Other information
The Coastal Zone centre is open seasonally. Dunluce Castle and visitor centre are open daily; admission fees apply.

Located on the ruggedly beautiful Antrim Coast and part of the Causeway Coast Area of Outstanding Natural Beauty, the walk from Portrush to the White Rocks takes you on a journey of geological discovery. From high-powered scientific debates to legends of lost towns, the coastline here is full of natural and cultural heritage.

The starting point of the walk is the Coastal Zone interpretation centre from where you will be able to get access to the adjacent rocks **(1)**. It was at this location that a battle raged between two opposing groups of geologists in the late 18th century. The Neptunists believed that all rocks precipitated from sea water whereas the Plutonists believed that some rocks were formed from molten rock (magma). The Neptunists were gaining increasing support especially when the rocks here at Portrush that were thought to have formed from magma, were found to contain the coiled-shell ammonites, creatures that would have lived in the sea. However, careful field observations found that the rocks here were in fact marine sediments baked hard after coming into contact with molten rock (found directly beneath the rocks here at Portrush) so the Plutonists were right after all.

Follow the coastal path east until you reach Curran Strand and walk along the beach with the sand dunes on your right. As you look out to sea you will see the Skerries **(2)**. This small group of rocks off the coast are part of a sill, that formed when magma squeezed between horizontal layers of rock, where it cooled and hardened to form rocks called dolerite and gabbro. This sill is in the shape of a saucer and underlies a good deal of Portrush.

Carry on until you see some white rocks. These are a type of sedimentary rock called limestone **(3)**. This pure form of limestone is commonly called chalk and is made up of the shelly remains of billions of microscopic organisms called coccoliths. These creatures thrived in the warm, shallow waters of an ancient sea that covered Northern Ireland some 80 million years ago. When they died, the skeletons of the coccoliths sank onto the sea floor where they accumulated and became compressed into limestone.

If you look closely you will see that there are chunks of dark coloured rock called basalt both within the limestone and in places, making up the cliff face. The basalt was erupted as lava 60 million

CO. ANTRIM

Did you know?

The Skerries provided valuable shelter for the notorious Scottish pirate Tavish Dhú (or Black Tavish), who plundered ships making their way between Scotland and Ireland in the 14th Century.

years ago, and the presence of the basalt within the limestone indicates venting of hot gases caused by heat from the sill below.

At White Rocks follow the path uphill from the beach to the car park and up to the main road. Turn left and walk on to the footpath, where you will soon pass a disused quarry where the limestone below is overlain by the darker basalt **(4)**. The contact between the two is irregular and at one point you can see a large depression in the limestone that has been filled in with rounded boulders of basalt.

Continue along the footpath until you reach a bend just before a lay-by. On the left hand side you will see a 'blow hole' in the limestone where the force of the waves is weathering the rock away **(5)**. At the next bend there is an exposure of basalt in a bank on the opposite side of the road with a marked red layer **(6),** known as laterite, that represents a soil developed on top of a lava flow as it weathered under the sub-tropical climate of the time.

Continue on until you reach Magheracross car park **(7)** from where there are spectacular views west to the White Rocks and Curran Strand, Ramore Head and the Skerries, and beyond to Inishowen in Co. Donegal. To the east lies the Giant's Causeway and in clear weather the Isles of Islay and Jura in Scotland.

On the far side of the road you may once again notice the irregular contact between the limestone below and the basalt above. After the limestone formed and before the lava erupted, the landscape was exposed to the elements and was subjected to chemical weathering, similar to what is happening today in the Burren in Co. Clare. This has now been preserved beneath the basalt as the lava

Opposite: Aerial view of The Skerries with Ramore Head and Curran Strand in the background

flowed over the surface of the limestone protecting the shape of the landscape beneath.

Continue east towards Dunluce Castle (8), arguably one of the most spectacularly sited castles on the island of Ireland. Located on the edge of a basalt cliff, the site has had some form of defensive fort for at least the past 500 years, but almost all of the existing buildings date from the 16th and 17th centuries. Home to the McQuillan family and then later to the MacDonnell clan, the castle is thought to have been linked to a major town nearby known as the 'Lost Town of Dunluce' that was razed to the ground in the Irish uprising of 1641.

Follow the route back to the start point or alternatively, you can take a bus back to Portrush (see the Public Transport box).

Slemish Mountain

Slemish

GPS 54.882804, -6.104236 / Irish Grid D 21652 05551

Time: 1-2 hours
Distance: 3km (2 miles)
Grade: Strenuous
Type: Linear

Is it for me?
Suitable for adults

Start / Parking
Follow the brown signs from
Ballymena

Nearest town
Buckna

Refreshments
Broughshane

Public Toilets
Slemish car park

Public Transport
Ulsterbus service 129 arrives in
Buckna, which is a short walk from
the start

Maps
Larne Discoverer Sheet 9
Ballymena 1:50,000 Bedrock
Geology Sheet 20

Known for its link with Saint Patrick, Slemish Mountain
is an iconic site within the Antrim Coast and Glens Area
of Outstanding Natural Beauty. Standing proud from the
surrounding landscape and visible for miles around, this ancient
volcanic plug is a pilgrimage site for more reason than one.

What gives Slemish its characteristic shape, and why does it stand
proud from the surrounding area? Slemish Mountain is a volcanic
plug, created when molten rock (magma) hardened within a
volcano. Though no longer active, less than 60 million years ago it
spewed out lava over the surrounding area. It is the largest volcanic
plug on the island of Ireland and just one of several that would have
been active in the east of Northern Ireland at the time.

Park at the car park and read the information panels before
following the path to the summit of this landmark site.

The mountain itself is composed entirely of a dark coloured rock
called dolerite that would have formed when magma cooled and
crystallised at a shallow depth within the volcano. Dolerite is harder
than the surrounding rocks and as a result does not erode as
readily, thus its prominent position within the landscape.

The surrounding rocks are called basalt, which also formed from
molten rock, as flows of lava that spread out over the landscape
from fissures. Fissure eruptions occur from linear volcanic vents,
usually a few metres wide and many kilometres long, and usually
without any explosive activity. These sorts of eruptions produce
huge amounts of lava that cover large areas of land and are known
as flood basalts. It is this process that formed the entire Antrim
Plateau some 60 million years ago.

Dolerite is the medium-grained equivalent of basalt, meaning that
it has exactly the same composition but the crystals are larger and
can be seen with a hand lens (unlike basalt). Both rocks are known
as 'basic' rocks and are dominated by the minerals plagioclase
feldspar and pyroxene.

Legend has it that Saint Patrick, enslaved as a young man, was
brought to Slemish where he herded sheep on the slopes. During
his time here, Patrick learnt to speak the Irish language and after
six years of contemplation and solitude, is thought to have escaped

Did you know?

Firey volcanic eruptions like those that took place 60 million years ago in Northern Ireland and led to the formation of the flood basalts of the Antrim Plateau are presently seen in Iceland.

captivity after hearing voices telling him to bring Christianity to the Irish people.

Slemish lies at the end of the 35km (22 miles) long Antrim Hills Way, a two-day way-marked route that starts in the historic village of Glenarm. The walk comprises five different sections, each of which can be walked independently. The entire walk crosses some of the most scenic upland areas in the Antrim Glens and provides uninterrupted views across the sea to Scotland. The majority of the walk travels across the top of the basalts of the Antrim Plateau, exposed at several locations along the way. One of the most fascinating sites is Scawt Hill, a volcanic plug that is of particular interest as the magma that formed it, interacted with the white limestone that lies directly beneath producing a suite of minerals, including scawtite, that are found nowhere else on Earth.

The walk to the to the top of Slemish Mountain is clearly marked and while it is at times strenuous on the way up, the same route on the way back down is much easier, and allows you time to enjoy the surrounding scenery. There are excellent views from here of the Antrim and Scottish coasts to the east, while Ballymena town, the Sperrin Mountains and Lough Neagh can be seen to the west, and the Bann Valley can be seen to the north.

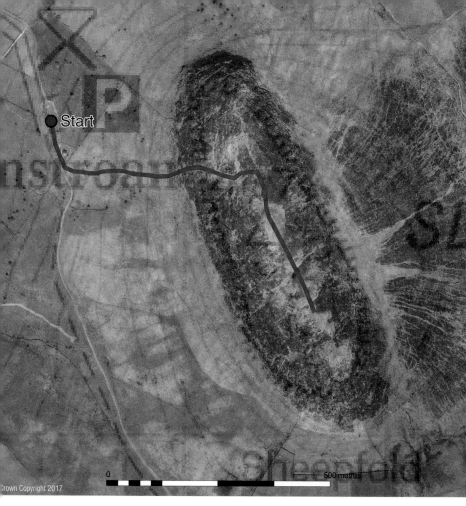

Opposite: The view toward the Sperrin Mountains from near the summit of Slemish

Right: Exposure of dolerite on the trail to Slemish

My black hills have never seen the sun rising,
Eternally they look north towards Armagh...

...My hills hoard the bright shillings of March
While the sun searches in every pocket.
They are my Alps and I have climbed the Matterhorn

From 'Shancoduff' by Patrick Kavanagh

Ballykeel Dolmen

Mullaghbane

GPS 54.108389, -6.478221 / Irish Grid H 99519 18779

Time: 4 to 5 hours
Distance: 13km (8 miles)
Grade: Leisurely
Type: Circular

Is it for me?
Suitable for adults, families with older children (8 years and older) and dog walkers

Start / Parking
Car parking at the Tí Cuhlainn Cultural Activity Centre in Mullaghbane

Nearest town
Mullaghbane

Refreshments
Mullaghbane

Public Toilets
Tí Cuhlainn Cultural Activity Centre

Public Transport
Ulsterbus Service 42 stops at Mullaghbane

Maps
Monaghan-Keady Discoverer Sheet 28

The Mullaghbane walk takes you through the dramatic landscapes of the Ring of Gullion Area of Outstanding Natural Beauty. Combined with a rich cultural and built heritage, the natural landscape of the region is one of Northern Ireland's best kept secrets.

You are following the route of the Poet's Trail - Ballykeel Loop, so from the car park look for the waymarkers and follow them for the duration of the walk.

Travelling north and then east, one of the first sites along the trail is a small disused quarry off to the left **(1)**. This quarry is in granite, and is the oldest rock that you will see on the walk, with an age of around 410 million years. This forms part of a great granite mass that stretches from here to Slieve Croob, north of Newcastle which formed as molten rock, or magma cooled deep below ground during a period of Earth history known as the Devonian. As the granite cooled it shrank and cracked to form the many fractures that you can see.

You will soon cross a bridge and begin to walk up a hill. During the climb notice that the rocks change from granite to a much darker rock called dolerite **(2)**.

As you continue to walk north along the path, Slieve Gullion is now on your right, with a series of hills straight ahead and to the left **(3)**. These form part of a ring of hills that encircles Slieve Gullion, known as the Ring of Gullion. This feature formed around 60 million years ago as Europe began to break away from North America, creating the North Atlantic Ocean. These Earth movements generated huge amounts of heat, causing magma (or molten rock) to rise from beneath the surface. However, the Ring of Gullion itself was produced when the magma chamber was no longer able to support the weight from above. As the chamber collapsed, it created cracks around its edge that molten rock was then able to squeeze into. This molten rock has now hardened and forms the 'ring' of rock that we see today.

Slieve Gullion formed slightly after the ring dyke and is what is known as a sheeted igneous intrusion. This means that it is composed of layers of igneous rock that were intruded into the pre existing country rock.

Did you know?

Tí Cuhlainn translates as the 'House of Culann' and refers to Culann a legendary blacksmith and armourer that lived on Slieve Gullion. He is most famous for his fierce watchdog that was slain by Sétanta. After killing the hound, Sétanta became known as Cu Chulainn or 'The Hound of Culann' and is perhaps the most famous hero of Irish mythology.

Continue north until you see the Ballykeel Dolmen **(4)**. This stone structure, originally covered by a mound of stones or cairn, dates back over 5,000 years to the Neolithic period. The dolmen (or portal tomb) would have been built as a burial site for someone of great importance, and its location on elevated ground highlights the fact that this structure was built to be seen for miles around.

As the route swings south you will pass Mullaghbane Lough **(5)**, with Slievebrack Mountain lying directly ahead. Slievebrack Mountain provides us with yet more evidence of volcanic activity as it is the site of one of many volcanic vents in the vicinity. During volcanism, gas would have built up creating huge amounts of pressure that eventually escaped through such vents. Such explosive activity can be compared to the shaking of a bottle of fizzy drink and then opening it, to find the liquid 'erupting' out of the bottle. As the volcanic gases escaped they would have ripped through the surrounding rock, breaking up the material in its path.

Continue following the waymarkers until you return to the start of the walk at Mullaghbane.

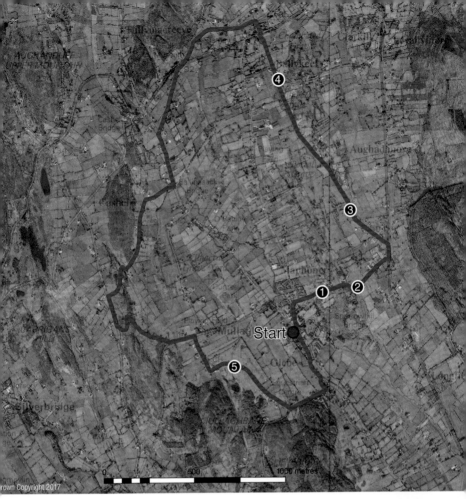

Opposite: View of the Ring of Gullion

Right: Walkers enjoying the gorse in full bloom in the Ring of Gullion AONB

Ring of Gullion

Slieve Gullion

GPS 54.105987, -6.424041 / Irish Grid J 03068 18590

Time: 5 to 6 hours
Distance: 13km (8 miles)
Grade: Strenuous
Type: Circular

Is it for me?
Suitable for adults

Start / Parking
Car parking at Slieve Gullion Forest
Park, signposted off the B113
Forkhill to Meigh Road

Nearest town
Meigh

Refreshments
Slieve Gullion Courtyard

Public Toilets
Slieve Gullion Courtyard

Public Transport
Ulsterbus service 443 (Slieve
Gullion Rambler) arrives at start
point during July and August

Maps
The Mournes Discoverer Sheet 29
Monaghan-Keady Discoverer
Sheet 28
1:250,000 Northern Ireland Solid
Geology

Other information
For families visiting the area there
is a children's playground available
at the start of walk. Slieve Gullion
Courtyard includes picnic areas, a
nature walk and wildfowl pond.

Steeped in legend, Slieve Gullion is perhaps one of the most
under explored areas in the whole of Northern Ireland yet one of
the most beautiful as its designation as an Area of Outstanding
Natural Beauty suggests. Its rugged scenery and past make it
a paradise for those who want to find out more about our links
with the land.

Starting from the car park at the Slieve Gullion Courtyard, follow
the signs for the Forest Drive west and continue on, ignoring any
tracks leading off the road, until you reach a second car park.

From the southern slopes of Slieve Gullion there are splendid
views to the south, east and west of Slieve Gullion. You will notice
a distinct ring of hills surrounds Slieve Gullion, known as the Ring
of Gullion that formed from the solidification of molten rock, or
magma that fed volcanic activity in this area some 60 million years
ago during the Palaeogene period.

As you approach the car park there are some interesting rocks on
the right hand side of the road **(1)**. There has been much scientific
debate as to how these light and dark rocks, and indeed Slieve
Gullion, came to be.

From the car park, follow the way-marked trail that leads to the
summit of Slieve Gullion where there are spectacular views and
a mound of stones known as a cairn **(2)**. Locally referred to as
'Calliagh Bera's House', this cairn is the highest surviving passage
tomb in Ireland and probably dates back to the Neolithic period.

Continue northwards passing Lough Calliagh Bera **(3)** into which,
according to legend, Finn McCool was lured after being enchanted
by a local witch. After bathing in the lake he emerged as a wizened
old man. To this day there is a local superstition that believes
should you bathe in the lake, your hair will turn white.

Keep travelling northwards, uphill, following the waymarkers. At
the first marker a knoll of rock juts out on the left hand side of the
path **(4)**. This dark-coloured rock is dolerite, an igneous rock that
formed as magma that cooled and crystallised within the Earth's
crust. Near-horizontal sheets of dolerite are interbanded with a light
coloured igneous rock called granophyre. Together they make up
Slieve Gullion giving it a somewhat stepped profile.

Did you know?

Cam Lough (or Cam Loch) translates from the Irish as 'crooked lake' due to its characteristic shape. The name of the nearby village of Camlough has been wrongly translated as meaning the same, but it is actually an Anglicisation of Camlaigh meaning 'crooked mountain'.

Initially scientists thought that Slieve Gullion was made up of altered layers of lava that were erupted from volcanoes. However following significant scientific debate the more favoured explanation is that the layers of darker dolerite and lighter granophyre cooled in a magma chamber within the Earth's crust and never erupted as lava at the surface.

Continue on the path downhill, leading to a track and eventually to a road. Turn right and continue until you reach the Ballintemple Viewpoint from where you will see the elongate Cam Lough **(5)**. Sitting astride a crack, or fault in the Earth's crust, Cam Lough is a good example of a ribbon lake, a long narrow lake that forms in a trough that has been carved out by ice. The presence of a fault here created a weakness in the landscape making it easier for the glaciers during the last ice age to scour away the rocks.

Continue downhill past Camlough Wood, Killevy Churches and Killevy Castle. Located at the foot of Slieve Gullion, the two churches at Killevy **(6)** date back to the 11th and the 15th centuries. The site itself was the site of an early monastery founded by St. Monina in 517 and was one of the most important monasteries for nuns in Medieval Ireland.

After the entrance to the castle, take the next right and then left to return to the start.

Start

Opposite: Slieve Gullion and the surrounding Ring of Gullion

Right: The Ring of Gullion Way is part of the much longer Ulster Way that extends through the province of Ulster

River Blackwater

Maghery

GPS 54.513048, -6.572657 / Irish Grid H 92432 63685

Time: 2 hours
Distance: 8km (5 miles)
Grade: Easy
Type: Circular

Is it for me?
Suitable for adults, families with older and younger children and dog walkers

Start / Parking
Car park at Maghery Country Park

Nearest town
Maghery

Refreshments
Service station at Portadown Road (off M1 Junction 12)

Public Toilets
Maghery Social Club (12pm onwards)

Public Transport
Ulsterbus service 75

Maps
Armagh Discoverer Sheet 19
1:250,000 Northern Ireland Solid Geology

Other Information
Boat trips run to Coney Island on the first Sunday of each month May to August from Maghery Country Park from 1.30pm – 4.30pm. Other times and visits can be arranged including private trips. There is a children's playground at Maghery County Park.

Skirting the south-western shore of Lough Neagh, this gentle walk takes in the sights, sounds and smells of the rich rural heritage that this area has to offer.

The walk begins at Maghery Country Park from where there is access to Lough Neagh, the largest freshwater lake in the UK and Ireland. Lough Neagh is a huge depression in the landscape that has been a site for the natural deposition of sediments for millions of years. Some of these sediments have now turned into lignite, which is a type of soft brown coal that formed from the alteration of plant matter that would have accumulated here in a swamp-type environment when this area was at sub-tropical latitudes about 25 million years ago.

Starting from the car park at Maghery Country Park, walk back to the road and turn left. Once you reach the main road turn right. Follow this road for approximately 1km and then take the first road on the left (Derryane Road) **(1)**.

The area is known for its boat building history and traditional crafts known as currachs have been built here since early Christian times. These wooden framed vessels would have been covered with stretched animal skin or hides and were the dominant form of transport on inland waters in Ireland.

The small, rounded hills that you pass along the way are known as drumlins. They formed as ice moved over the landscape during the last ice age. Throughout the ice age, which stretches back 2–3 million years and continues, icesheets have spread out from Lough Neagh in all directions on many occasions. Evidence of cold arctic conditions has been found around the shores of the Lough in the form of woolly mammoth remains such as teeth, tusks and bones.

Apple orchards are a common site in Co. Armagh and were first planted by English settlers who arrived here during the Plantation of Ulster in the 17th century. However the history of the apple in Co. Armagh is said to be traced back to the days of St. Patrick when the Saint is said to have planted an apple tree at the ancient settlement of Ceangoba east of Armagh city.

Did you know?

The word drumlin comes from the Irish 'droimnín' meaning 'little ridge'. Drumlins are just one of several glacial features whose names originate in the Irish language and are now used internationally.

Keep following this road as it takes a sharp bend to the left after approximately another 1km. Walk on until you reach a T-junction and turn left onto the Derrylileagh Road **(2)**.

The townland of Derrylileagh contained part of a causeway that stretched from Coney Island (visible from the shore of Lough Neagh at Maghery) all the way to Armagh, a distance of some 8km (13 miles). The causeway, known as St Patrick's Trail, was constructed from oak planks from trees that would have been plentiful in the area in early Christian times. The trail was used to link the monastery of Saint Peter and Paul in Armagh with an outlying monastery at Maghery.

Stay on this road for approximately 2km and at the T-junction turn left onto the main Maghery Road **(3)**. There is a footpath on the opposite side of the road that can be accessed at this point. Keep on this footpath and follow the signs back to Maghery Country Park.

As you return to the car park, you will see the River Blackwater as it enters Lough Neagh. Lough Neagh drains over 40% of Northern Ireland's surface and the Blackwater is one of the six major rivers that feed in to the lake. The Blackwater is important as it is one of only two rivers that contain the white-clawed crayfish, and it is also a significant recreational resource as it is navigable as far as Blackwatertown.

Start

Landing Stage

Maghery Country Park

Maghery

❶

❷ 1000 metres

❸

0

Crown Copyright 2017

Opposite: One of many apple
orchards in Co. Armagh

Right: Coney Island, Lough Neagh

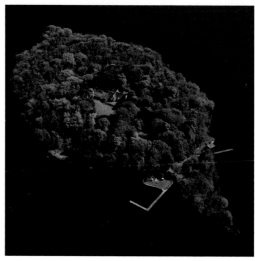

And you are riding not on a road, nor in a park, nor e
in Spring, down solemn avenues of beech and across
of snow-white cherry trees, past roaring waterfalls a
windy slopes alight gorse bushes, and across the sh
giddy ridges and down, down, down again into wild

From 'The Lion, the Witch and the Wardrobe' by C.S.

n the downs, but right across Narnia,
y glades of oak, through wild orchards
ossy rocks and echoing caverns, up
s of heathery mountains and along
s and out into acres of blue flowers.

Scrabo Tower

Scrabo

GPS 54.577522, -5.718336 / Irish Grid J 47516 72318

Time: 2 hours
Distance: 5km (3 miles)
Grade: Leisurely
Type: Circular

Is it for me?
Suitable for adults, families with older and younger children and dog walkers

Start / Parking
Scrabo Country Park car park, signposted off A21 between Comber and Newtownards

Nearest town
Comber/Newtownards

Refreshments
Comber/Newtownards

Public Toilets
Scrabo Country Park car park

Public Transport
Ulsterbus service 5A and 5B

Maps
Belfast Discoverer Sheet 15
1:250,000 Northern Ireland Solid Geology

Scrabo Hill and Tower are landmark features at the head of Strangford Lough. Seen from miles around, they offer wonderful views of County Down and the Mourne Mountains. However, it is the area's industrial heritage that provides windows into the very distant past.

The walk begins at the car park for Scrabo Country Park that is signposted from the A21 Comber to Newtownards road. From the car park, cross the road and head up the tarmac path towards Scrabo Tower. The tower was built in 1857 as a memorial to the 3rd Marquess of Londonderry, Charles Stewart, for his contribution to the famine relief effort that had devastated Ireland only a decade previously.

Take the first path to the right (signposted for South Quarry) and walk through the picnic area and across to the path on the other side. As you descend you will see glimpses of pale pink rock forming the quarry face. Carry on until you reach the interpretive panel **(1)**.

The South Quarry reveals a history that goes back as far as 250 million years to the Triassic period and a time when Northern Ireland would have been in a similar position to the Sahara Desert. The pale pink rock that you can see in horizontal layers is sandstone and would have formed in such a desert. Between the sandstone are two layers of much darker grey rock called dolerite. These layers are known as sills and formed as molten rock (or magma) was 'injected' in between the horizontal layers of sandstone about 60 million years ago.

Continue down the path until you reach the quarry entrance **(2)**. Please be careful and don't approach the quarry faces as there may be loose rocks. On the left hand side as you enter the quarry is a vertical wall of dolerite. Instead of being squeezed between layers like the sills, this would have been squeezed vertically up a fracture, or crack in the rock and is known as a dyke.

The majority of the quarry is sandstone, and has been used in a number of prominent buildings in nearby Newtownards as well as being the building stone for the Albert Memorial Clock in Belfast. If you look closely you will see some chocolate brown coloured rock called mudstone between the sandstone. This rock is also

Did you know?

The rocks at Scrabo

contain fossilised

footprints of a four-

legged reptile called

Chirotherium lomasi, a

very distant relative of

the crocodile, that would

have roamed over the

landscape here around

250 million years ago.

the product of desert conditions but it would have been laid down during flash floods that would have periodically washed across the landscape. The mudstone reveals some wonderful features such as mud cracks, ripples and has even preserved footprints of a long extinct reptile.

Leave the quarry, turn left and continue on the path. Scrabo Hill stands proudly above the surrounding landscape and the reason for this is that the hill itself is capped with a layer of dolerite that has acted as a protective barrier against weathering and erosion. During the last ice age, when ice sheets slowly crept across the entire Northern Irish landscape, the force of the ice removed the surrounding softer sandstone, leaving the resistant dolerite behind. This feature is known as a crag and tail.

Take the path to the left that will lead you to a number of smaller quarry faces (3). These would have all been worked for their sandstone and the path that you have just come down would have been the course of the tramways used to remove stone for transportation elsewhere. Scrabo sandstone has been quarried since Anglo-Norman times with one of the earliest buildings constructed from the sandstone being the 13th century monastery at Greyabbey.

Return on the track you came in on, past the South Quarry, and back to the car park. If you have the energy, make the trip to the top of Scrabo Hill where you can see the dolerite exposed and notice the characteristic joints or cracks that would have formed as the rock cooled (4).

Return on the path you came and walk back to the car park.

Start

500 metres

Crown Copyright 2017

Opposite: View down the Ards Peninsula and Strangford Lough from the top of Scrabo

Right: Horizontal layers of igneous rock (sills) exposed in the wall of the South Quarry

Dundrum Bay and Slieve Donard

Slieve Donard

GPS 54.205698, -5.894562 / Irish Grid J 37361 30586

Time: 4 to 5 hours
Distance: 13km (8 miles)
Grade: Strenuous
Type: Circular

Is it for me?
Suitable for adults

Start / Parking
Car parking at Donard Park, Newcastle

Nearest town
Newcastle

Refreshments
Newcastle

Public Toilets
Donard Park

Public Transport
A number of Ulsterbus services arrive in Newcastle Bus Station which is 1km (0.6 miles) from the start of the walk. These include the 34 (Bryansford/Slievenaman), 17 (Downpatrick-Newry), 18, 20, 518 & 237 (Belfast), 26B (Ballynahinch-Lisburn), 32 (Banbridge), and 37 (Kilkeel). Ulsterbus service 405 (Mourne Rambler) operates from May to August.

Maps
The Mournes Discoverer Sheet 29
The Mournes (including Slieve Croob) Activity Map

This stunning walk circumnavigates Slieve Donard, at 850m the highest mountain in Northern Ireland, and offers an insight into the once thriving granite industry of the area as well as superb views out over the surrounding countryside and Irish Sea.

Leave the car park, head south-west towards the mountain and follow the Glen River uphill through the woodland. As you walk, look down at the river bed as well as at many of the rocks on the path **(1)**. These are a type of rock called greywacke, a form of sandstone that would have been deposited on the floor of an ancient ocean over 420 milllion years ago during the Silurian period.

At the second bridge, there are a series of waterfalls and a gorge that owe their existence to the presence of igneous dykes **(2)**. These formed as injections of molten rock (or magma) into the existing solid rock (or country rock) around 55 million years ago.

Continue uphill through the forest of Scots and Corsican pine. The tranquil woodland habitat is home to red squirrels and pine martens and in late summer you may be lucky enough to spot a holly blue butterfly. Cross to the opposite side of the river and after a short distance a small stream joins from the right **(3)**. Just upstream from here is a flat sheet of water passing over a smooth rock face, marking the boundary of the greywacke and the grey and white granite that makes up this part of the Mournes.

There are five different types of granite in the Mournes, but they all formed in a similar way deep within the Earth's crust as molten rock. Around 60 million years ago, the single tectonic plate that carried the European and North American continents began to tear apart, leading to the formation of the North Atlantic Ocean. As the Earth's crust stretched and thinned, large volumes of rock were melted at depth generating reservoirs of magma. This magma never erupted but cooled underground and hardened to form granite. Millennia of erosion and weathering have now exposed this subterranean magma chamber at the surface.

Continue on the forest road and onto a rough track heading up towards the mountains, with thick forest on the right, until a gate and a stile is reached. Cross the stile and follow the track above the river for about 2km, heading towards the saddle between

Did you know?

The landscapes of the Mourne Mountains are said to have inspired Belfast-born C.S. Lewis to create the magical world of Narnia after holidaying in Rostrevor on the edge of the Mournes as a child.

Slieve Donard and Commedagh. As you walk, you will see a small round building on the opposite bank of the river **(4)**. This is an ice-house, built by the Annesley family whose estate stretched from Slieve Croob to Slieve Donard, taking in Castlewellan and part of Newcastle. The ice-house was used to store perishable foods prior to the invention of the refrigerator.

Travel uphill until you reach the Mourne Wall, built between 1904 and 1922 to mark the boundary of land owned by the Belfast Water Commissioners. Turn left at the Mourne Wall and continue on until you reach the summit of Slieve Donard **(5)**. From the summit the view extends north towards Scrabo Hill and the Ards Peninsula. The view south looks over the Mourne coastal plain to the Cooley Mountains in Co. Louth.

There are two prehistoric cairns on the summit, the larger of which is said to have been a hermitage for the local Christian missionary, St. Donard after whom the mountain is named.

Retrace your steps but on the opposite side of the Mourne Wall. Take the path to the left, which is known as the Brandy Pad, along which wine, tobacco, tea and of course, brandy were smuggled in the 18th century.

After 2km, the path passes by a large quarry where Mourne granite was worked **(6)**. Granite would have been quarried from here and transported to the coast at Newcastle via a mineral tramway, seen just off to the right. Mourne granite is world-famous and has been used as paving stones in cities such as London and New York and has also been used to make the base of the 9/11 memorial in New York by local Kileel stonemasons.

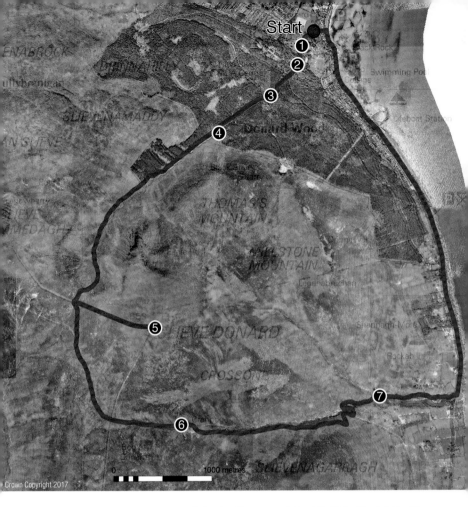

Start
① ② ③ ④ ⑤ ⑥ ⑦

0   1000 metres

© Crown Copyright 2017

Opposite: The ice-house on the climb of Slieve Donard

Follow the old quarry track downhill with the Bloody Bridge River to your left. After crossing a stile and a footbridge, the Bloody Bridge River is joined by the Glen Fofanny River. Just downstream from this is the contact point between the granite and the much older greywacke **(7)**. When the granite was injected (or intruded) into the greywacke, the intense heat from the granite 'baked' the surrounding greywacke where they came into contact, causing its appearance to change (a process known as contact metamorphism). As you walk down stream you will see that the greywacke displays purplish and greenish stripes, and looks very different to the greywacke at the start of the walk.

Follow the path downhill until you reach the main A2 Newcastle to Kilkeel Road at Bloody Bridge. Turn left and follow the road for 3km back to Newcastle and the starting point at Donard Park.

Rocks of the Kearney Siltstone Formation

Kearney

GPS 54.385231, -5.475612 / Irish Grid J 63973 51458

Time: 1 to 2 hours
Distance: 5km (3 miles)
Grade: Moderate
Type: Circular

Is it for me?
Suitable for adults, families with older and younger children and dog walkers

Start / Parking
Car parking at Knockinelder Bay

Nearest town
Portaferry

Refreshments
Portaferry

Public Toilets
Kearney village

Maps
Strangford Discoverer Sheet 21
1:250,000 Northern Ireland Solid Geology

Kearney is located at the southern end of the Ards Peninsula and is part of the Strangford Lough and Lecale Area of Outstanding Natural Beauty. This tranquil coastal walk offers a glimpse into the long and fascinating partnership between the landscape and the people who live here.

Starting from the car park at Knockinelder Bay take the short path to the beach and turn left. The rocks that can be seen along this coast are a type of sandstone known as greywacke. These formed at the bottom of a deep ocean, many thousands of kilometres wide called Iapetus, about 440 million years ago during the Silurian period **(1)**. The Iapetus Ocean separated the northern part of the island of Ireland from the southern part; the northern half would have been joined with parts of North America, Greenland and Scotland whilst the southern part was joined with England, Wales and eastern Canada.

As the Earth's plates slowly changed direction, the Iapetus Ocean began to shrink as the two continents moved closer together. The rocks of the Ards Peninsula are positioned north of where the United Kingdom and Ireland finally joined. This join, or suture, runs through Ireland from Clogherhead in Co. Louth on the east coast, to the Shannon Estuary in Co. Limerick on the south-west coast.

When the greywackes were deposited they would have been laid down horizontally. The forces involved when these two landmasses collided caused the rocks to deform and fold. Numerous examples of folds with steeply dipping beds (layers) of greywacke can be seen at Kearney.

From this point, you will be able to see Quintin Castle **(2)**. This Anglo-Norman castle was built in 1184 by John de Courcy and is one of many Norman tower houses around Strangford Lough. The proximity of this part of Northern Ireland to Scotland and its location as a peninsula meant that it was frequently invaded, so defensive structures are common.

Continue eastwards along the coast where you will see many more examples of folded, crumpled and even upturned rocks **(3)**. As you look out to sea, on a clear day the Isle of Man will be visible. Culturally, there are very strong links between here and the Isle of Man as it was the birthplace of John de Courcy's wife Affreca, who

Did you know?

Stories have been told of a 'she-cruiser' that was crewed entirely by women that set out to fish in the surrounding waters, and if true would have been very unusual in such a male-dominated industry during the 19th Century.

later founded the Cistercian monastery of Greyabbey on the west side of the Ards Peninsula.

As the path swings towards the northeast, the fishing village of Kearney will come into view **(4)**. This 19th century settlement has been restored by the National Trust and is a reminder of the many fishing communities that would have existed all along the Ards Peninsula. The lack of roads before the 19th century meant that many of these villages had more contact with Scotland by sea than they did with other parts of the peninsula.

From Kearney take the main road back to the car park at Knockinelder. As you go you will pass a windmill **(5)** that would have been used to roll oats and grind wheat and is one of hundreds of windmills that can be found all across the peninsula.

As you approach Knockinelder, you will see a small hill from where the village gets its name (An Cnoc is Irish for 'hill'). This hill and others around Kearney are formed from sands and gravels that were deposited at the ends of a melting glacier (known as moraine).

Keep on this road until you return to the car park at Knockinelder Bay.

Start

① ② ③ ④ ⑤

Kearney Point

Wee Rock

0   500 metres

© Crown Copyright 2017

Opposite: A millstone on display in Kearney village

Right: The National Trust owned Kearney village is an example of what was once a traditional Irish fishing community

The reef-knolls of the Fermanagh Marlbank and the C
And the great deltaic sandbar of Cuilcagh stood out ir
Coming from the far-east while a membrane of mist
Still clung to the semi-submerged headlands of the is

From 'Decommissioned' by Seamus O' hUltacháin

n Burren
e morning sunshine

ds of Lower Lough MacNean

Cuilcagh Mountain from the limestone pavement at Gortmaconnell

Gortmaconnell

GPS 54.254771, -7.802997 / Irish Grid H 12838 34018

Time: 2 to 3 hours
Distance: 8km (5 miles)
Grade: Leisurely
Type: Linear

Is it for me?
Suitable for adults and families with older children (8 years or older)

Start / Parking
Car parking at Legg, clearly signposted from the Marlbank Road

Nearest town
Florencecourt / Blacklion

Refreshments
Marble Arch Caves Visitor Centre

Public Toilets
Marble Arch Caves Visitor Centre

Maps
Lough Allen Discoverer Sheet 26
1:250,000 Northern Ireland Solid Geology

Other Information
The Marble Arch Caves Visitor Centre is open from March to October. Tours of the showcaves are available for a fee but access to the visitor centre is free of charge.

Located in Cuilcagh Mountain Park, and part of the much larger Marble Arch Caves Unesco Global Geopark, the walk at Gortmaconnell is one of the lesser known parts of this picturesque area. Showcasing the wonderful geology and landscape features of this region, the walk at Gortmaconnell follows the trail of the Owenbrean River, one of three rivers that feed into the Marble Arch Caves.

Park in the small lay-by at the gate marked as Gortmaconnell, just off the Marlbank Road. Alternatively you can park at the Marble Arch Caves Visitor Centre and walk the short distance to the beginning of the walk. Go through the gate and after a short while you will see a sign marked as Gortmaconnell Rock. Follow this sign and keep walking east until you reach the highest point.

Gortmaconnell Rock **(1)** is a hill made up of limestone that formed about 340 million years ago from the shells of sea creatures as well as lime-rich muds at the bottom of a shallow tropical sea. There are a number of other limestone hills visible from this point that would have been mounds of lime-rich mud on the bottom of this ancient sea floor. Gortmaconnell Rock, although similar to these 'mudmounds' is made up of flat-lying limestone layers, or beds, and was carved into its current shape during the last ice age.

From the top of Gortmaconnell Rock there are fine views to the north and across the Marlbank towards the Burren Forest in Co. Cavan in the west. You can also clearly see Upper and Lower Lough MacNean. The valley that Lough MacNean now occupies was carved by a series of ice sheets during the last 2–3 million years. As the ice sheets melted, global sea level rose resulting in flooding of major valleys such as this one. The lake is now divided in two by deposits of sand and gravel (or moraines), left behind when the glaciers melted, forming a natural bridge.

Go back down hill and turn left to rejoin the main track. As you walk you will see exposures of limestone on either side **(2)**, some of which display much darker patches and layers. This is a material called chert and would have formed at the same time as the limestone 340 million years ago. Chert is very similar to flint and can be broken to form a very sharp edge. For this reason it was used by Mesolithic settlers to make hunting tools such as arrows and axes.

Did you know?

The 'Whale Rock' is a large boulder dumped on the landscape when the icesheets melted. It has been split by early settlers in the region, with the purpose of using it is a building stone. The rock didn't split in the right place so it is still in its original location where it is said to resemble a whale.

You will see the Owenbrean River on your right hand side **(3)**. Depending on what time of year you visit, this riverbed may be completely dry or it could be a gushing torrent! The reason for this is that limestone dissolves in weak acidic water leading to the formation of underground channels and caves that provide an alternative path for the river. When the river is in low flow (mainly during the summer), the river sinks below ground leaving the river bed completely exposed.

Walk on for approximately 1km to where the river takes a sharp deviation. This is an indication of the geological feature known as the Cuilcagh Dyke **(4)**. This vertical sheet of solid rock would have formed at around the same time as the Giant's Causeway, around 60 million years ago, when Europe was tearing apart from North America. Because of earth movement, huge amounts of magma, or molten rock were produced. In many cases the magma was forced up into cracks in the crust known as faults where it solidified to form dykes. The Cuilcagh Dyke has greatly influenced the water flow of the region, both above and below ground. The courses of the three main rivers on Cuilcagh Mountain all take sharp deviations when they cross the Cuilcagh Dyke, reflecting the variation between the rock types of the dyke and the surrounding limestone.

If water levels are low, it is possible to see the Cuilcagh Dyke exposed in the river bank. It is easy to spot as it displays onion-skin weathering (so called as the surface of the rocks flake off in layers similar to an onion) and is a rusty red colour due to the presence of iron. You may also be able to see where the limestone has been in direct contact with the hot molten rock, and has been 'cooked'. The

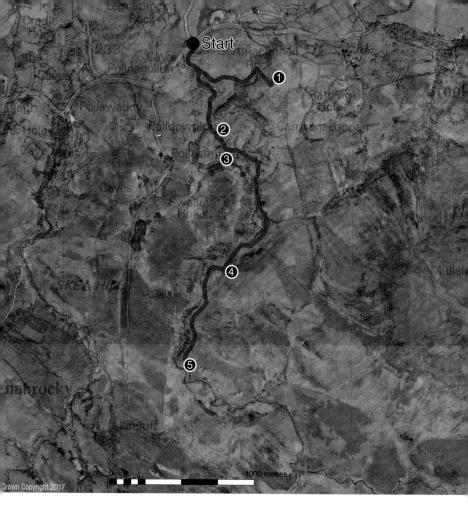

Opposite: Whale Rock

limestone nearest to the dyke looks very different to the limestone that you have seen previously.

Continue on up the track and if the river is in low water conditions this may be the first time that you will be able to see, or at least hear, the flow of the water. The reason for this is that the rock type beneath your feet has changed from limestone to sandstone which does not dissolve and so the water flows over rather than through it.

Continue on until you reach the very end of the track **(5)**, where there is a small exposure of pale yellow sandstone. If you look at some of the broken blocks you may be able to see ripples on the surface, similar to those that you might see on the beach. These ripples formed in exactly the same way, over 330 million years ago, when this area was a tidal flat similar to that found in the Persian Gulf.

Return to the track and make your way back to the car park, enjoying the stunning views as you make your way downhill.

Pollnagollum Cave

Pollnagollum

GPS 54.339247, -7.814884 / Irish Grid H 12039 43419

Time: 2 hours
Distance: 7km (4.5 miles)
Grade: Easy
Type: Circular

Is it for me?
Suitable for adults, families with older and younger children and dog walkers

Start / Parking
Lay-by at entrance to Belmore Forest

Nearest town
Belcoo

Refreshments
Belcoo

Public Toilets
Cottage Lawn, Belcoo

Maps
Lower Lough Erne Discoverer Sheet 17
1:250,000 Northern Ireland Solid Geology

Located right in the heart of Fermanagh's cave country, and part of the Marble Arch Caves Unesco Global Geopark, the Pollnagollum Cave walk takes you through the scenic Belmore Forest offering stunning views from Belmore Mountain as well as rare glimpses into this secretive underground landscape.

Starting from the lay-by at the entrance to Belmore Forest, follow the waymarkers that will guide you along the route.

Moving south, the first feature that you will come across is the abandoned quarry **(1)** just after the entrance to the forest. Coolarkan Quarry is just one of many in west Fermanagh that were worked for limestone, principally for road construction. This limestone formed over 340 million years ago during the Carboniferous period when the island of Ireland would have been located somewhere near the equator and covered by a shallow, tropical sea. The rock itself is made up from lime-rich mud from the sea floor as well as the fossilised remains of animals that would have lived in such a sea. Please remember not to approach the quarry face as it may be unstable.

As you continue along the path you will reach what is undoubtedly the highlight of the walk, Pollnagollum Cave **(2)**. A viewing platform allows you to see the entrance as well as a powerful waterfall that cascades from the top of the 12 metre high limestone cliff. At this point in the walk you are actually standing inside a collapsed cave, with the edge of the waterfall being the former roof. Caves form in limestone as it is dissolved by weakly acidic water over many hundreds and thousands of years. When a cave can no longer support its roof it simply collapses as is the case here.

Pollnagollum translates from the Irish as 'hole of the doves', and this rather romantic sounding cave was the precursor to the show caves of the Marble Arch Caves. Used during Victorian times as a visitor attraction, you may be able to see the worn remains of steps that take you into the mouth of the cave. Once inside, Pollnagollum isn't very long, contains few cave features and is rather unimpressive, but given the lack of technology available at the time, this would have undoubtedly been an exciting destination.

Return to the track and continue on the walk, meandering uphill until you reach the upland of Belmore Mountain **(3)**. From here

Did you know?

Pollnagollum cave was used as the setting for Beric Dondarrion's hideout in Game of Thrones. Very little filming was done on site but a complete replica of the cave was constructed and used for filming at the Titanic Studios in Belfast.

there are spectacular views of Cuilcagh Mountain and Lower Lough MacNean to the south and Brougher Mountain to the east. The Carboniferous rocks in this region are more often than not arranged in horizontal layers like those of a cake. Limestone forms the bottom layer and is followed by layers of mudstone and sandstone that formed as a huge river delta built out into the sea.

Belmore Mountain, just like Cuilcagh Mountain, has a characteristic flat-topped profile. In the past the horizontal layers of rocks of Belmore Mountain would have continued across to Cuilcagh Mountain, however, weathering and erosion, particularly due to the movement of glaciers during the last ice age have since carved out a huge u-shaped valley leaving Cuilcagh and Belmore mountains as 'islands' of rock.

As you continue on through the forest, you may be lucky enough to spot Irish hares. Larger than rabbits, adult hares have black tips on their ears and their long back legs give them a distinctive walk or 'lope'. This rare mammal is native to Ireland (unlike rabbits that were brought here in the 12th century by the Normans) and is arguably our oldest surviving mammal having been present in Ireland since before the last ice age.

Continue along the walk until you return to the start point.

Start

① ②

③

Polinagollum Cave

Coolarkan

Belmore Forest

curragh

0   500   1000 metres

rown Copyright 2017

Opposite: A professionally led
exploration of Pollnagollum cave

Right: Walking in Belmore Forest

Chapel ruins at Castle Caldwell

Rossergole

GPS 54.492028, -7.975988 / Irish Grid H 01556 60408

Time: 1 hour
Distance: 4km (2.5 miles)
Grade: Easy
Type: Circular

Is it for me?
Suitable for adults, families with older and younger children and dog walkers

Start / Parking
Car parking at Castle Caldwell Forest Park

Nearest town
Belleek

Refreshments
Belleek

Public Toilets
Erne Gateway Centre, Belleek

Public Transport
Ulsterbus service 195/195H arrives at Scardans which is 500m from the start

Maps
Lower Lough Erne Discoverer Sheet 17
1:250,000 Northern Ireland Solid Geology

Other Information
The nearby Belleek Pottery visitor centre is open all year round

The Rossergole Forest Walk is located in the ever changing Castle Caldwell Forest on the shores of Lower Lough Erne within the Marble Arch Caves Unesco Global Geopark. It offers a rare chance to walk through a semi-natural woodland located in one of Northern Ireland's deceptively industrial landscapes.

Starting from the car park in Castle Caldwell Forest, follow the waymarkers east for the Rossergole Forest Walk, one of the three waymarked walks in the forest.

One of the first features you will come across is an industrial-scale lime kiln **(1)** that hints at the association of the Caldwell estate with the nearby Belleek Pottery. During the 1840s John Caldwell Bloomfield, the estate owner, ordered a geological survey of his lands and soon discovered all of the raw materials necessary to make pottery. One of these materials was limestone, that when fired in a lime kiln, converts into calcium oxide (or quicklime), vital in the production of white ware pottery. The first foundation stone of Belleek Pottery was laid in 1853 by Mrs Bloomfield from where it grew into the successful business that it is today.

Not too far from here are exposures of the oldest rocks in Northern Ireland, known as psammite. Formed around 650 million years ago, these ancient rocks would have probably originally formed as sandstone but have since been subjected to intense heat and pressure causing them to change into the metamorphic rock known as psammite. Within this ancient rock is another type of rock called pegmatite. This igneous rock is made up of large mineral crystals including feldspar which is another vital component in the manufacture of Belleek Pottery. Whilst all of the material for the pottery was originally sourced locally, sadly this is no longer the case and all of the raw materials are now imported.

As you continue on the walk you will reach Rossergole Point **(2)** the location of a strategic fort on the shores of Lower Lough Erne. The valley that Lower Lough Erne now occupies was carved out by glaciers as they moved out towards the Atlantic Ocean over the last 2 to 3 million years. As sea-level rose at the end of the last ice age, the breathtaking flooded landscape of Lower Lough Erne was formed.

Lower Lough Erne also played a significant part in World War 2, being home to No. 209 Squadron RAF. From their base at RAF

Did you know?

Castle Caldwell forest is said to be haunted by numerous ghosts, one of which is said to be the fiddler, Dennis McCabe. He was a favourite of the Caldwell family but drowned after falling off the family's barge. A stone violin was erected in his memory and can now be seen at the entrance to the forest.

Castle Archdale, planes could patrol the North Atlantic for German U-boats, gaining access to the Atlantic Ocean from the glacially carved valley occupied by Lower Lough Erne through the Atlantic Corridor.

The water level of Lower Lough Erne is now much lower than it would have been naturally. A series of water management schemes in both the 19th and 20th centuries have lowered the lake, exposing new land and leaving many of the lake-side features literally high and dry. The most recent lowering of the lake level occurred as a result of the construction of a hydroelectric power station in the 1950s in Ballyshannon, Co. Donegal. In order to increase the flow of water to the power station, the exposed sandstone in the bed of the river Erne in Belleek was altered with explosives resulting in an increased flow of water as well as lowering of the lake. Along the walk you might catch a glimpse of abandoned jetties used to transport goods to and from the estate that are now far from the water's edge and a reminder of the former water levels.

Returning to the car park you will pass the ruins of Castle Caldwell (3). Built in 1612 as part of the Plantation of Ulster it is just one of a series of Plantation castles in Co. Fermanagh. The exceptional natural landscapes of Co. Fermanagh have led to the formation of a huge number of waterways meaning that it has always been vulnerable to attack. Over the millennia many have tried and succeeded in attacking strategic points in the county including the Vikings, English invaders and neighbouring tribes.

Continue on the walk until you return to the car park.

Opposite: Looking out over Lower
Lough Erne

Right: Arriving at the jetty, Castle
Caldwell Forest

Roots dig deep
Landscape inherent
Words from stone
Dirt we inherit

'Inheritance' by Mark Cooper

Crockmore and Crockbrack Mountain

Crockbrack

GPS 54.816959, -6.831737 / Irish Grid H 75093 97201

Time: 4 hours
Distance: 13km (8 miles)
Grade: Strenuous
Type: Circular

Is it for me?
Suitable for adults

Start / Parking
Car park at chapel in Moneyneany

Nearest town
Moneyneany

Refreshments
Moneyneany

Public Toilets
Filling station in Draperstown

Maps
Sperrins Discoverer Sheet 13
1:250,000 Northern Ireland Solid
Geology

Hidden away in the heart of Northern Ireland, the dramatic Sperrin Mountains are a walker's paradise. The Crockbrack walk offers a diversity of landscapes on bleak mountain summits to the peaceful tranquillity of farmland on the valley floors. It is no wonder that this area has been designated as the Sperrin Area of Outstanding Natural Beauty.

Starting from the chapel car park, walk through the village and cross the bridge over the Douglas River before turning right up the Drumderg Road. Keep on this road for approximately 1km until you reach Crockataggart, and then follow the Ulster Way, going steeply uphill.

As you continue upwards on the path, the view behind you takes in Moydamlaght Forest on the slopes of Mullaghmore, Benbradagh near Dungiven, Binevenagh near Limavady and Inishowen in Co. Donegal **(1)**.

Staying on the same track, ignore the many paths to the left and continue upwards. Along the side of the track are large boulders, known as glacial erratics **(2),** that were transported here by ice during the last ice age.

As you reach the summit of Crockmore you will see extensive blanket bog deposits **(3)**, and a few kilometres away is the hidden mountain lake of Lough Ouske on the northern slopes of Slieveavaddy. Blanket bog is typically a few metres thick and generally forms in upland areas as a uniform cover of peat over the underlying bedrock. Globally, it is a very rare habitat and is home to a unique range of plants and animals.

After a short distance, the path forks so turn right at this point and walk towards to the summit of Crockbrack. Once you reach a fence, turn right and head towards the top. Turn left when you reach the fence that goes along the summit, crossing the stile, but continuing in the same direction.

There are fantastic views from Crockbrack **(4)** including Lough Fea and several other smaller round lakes. Lough Fea is located in an area of quite flat but boggy ground that formed as material was washed out from melting ice sheets at the end of the last ice age. The sand and gravels that form this area are an important local

Did you know?

The townland of Moneyneany gets its name from the Irish Móin na nIonadh that translates as 'bog of wonders'. Legend states that it was the location for ancient Irish warriors to learn their exercises and to perform great feats of magic.

resource and are extracted nearby. The majority of them are kettle lakes that formed where blocks of ice became detached from the main ice sheet. As the main ice sheet continued to melt the large blocks became buried by the resulting loose material such as sand and gravel. As the ice blocks melted, they left behind a hollow which in turn filled with water to become a kettle lake.

Follow the fence until you intersect another fence to the right (5). Follow this and descend from Crockbrack. There is very little bedrock seen here but halfway down the slope you will see an exposure of a metamorphic rock called schist. This rock is contorted or folded and this is evidence of the forces exerted during a period of collisions between continents that occurred near here about 465 million years ago. The schist would have originally been a sedimentary rock such as mudstone, siltstone or sandstone, but the extreme pressures and temperatures that it was subjected to altered, or metamorphosed, it into schist.

When you reach the bottom of the slope, continue straight on and upslope again, still keeping the fence to your left. After about 500m you will meet another two fences at a y-junction. Go over the stile and turn right and follow the path towards the summit of Craigbane.

The views from the summit of Craigbane (6) are exceptional and extend from south-east to north-east over Slieve Gallion, Draperstown, the Moyola Valley and Maghera. To the east you can see Lough Neagh, Lough Beg and the Bann Valley.

Continue following the path, going straight on as you reach any junctions. After crossing the bridge over the Dunlogan River you

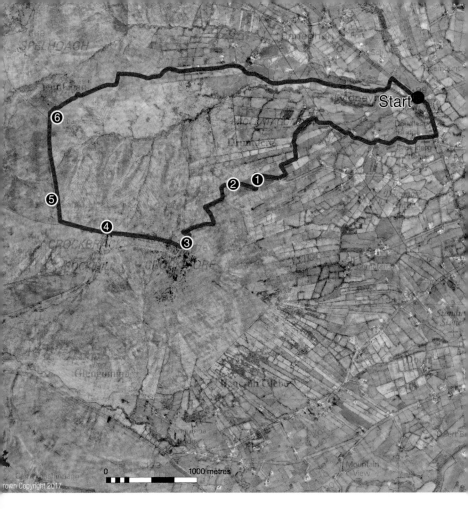

Start

① ② ③ ④ ⑤ ⑥

0   1000 metres

Crown Copyright 2017

Opposite: The rolling tops of the Sperrin Mountains as seen from the Crockbrack walk

Right: Folds seen in the schist on the descent from Crockbrack

come to the junction with the main Feeny to Moneyneany Road. Turn right to bring you back to the chapel car park.

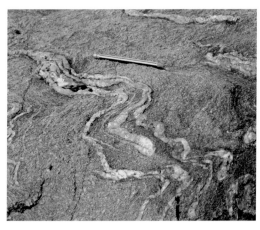

Binevenagh

Binevenagh

GPS 55.118293, -6.917782 / Irish Grid C 69044 30652

Time: 3 to 4 hours
Distance: 12km (7.5 miles)
Grade: Leisurely
Type: Circular

Is it for me?
Suitable for adults, families with older children (8 years or older), and dog walkers

Start / Parking
Car parking at Binevenagh Lake, signposted off the Bishop's Road between Coleraine and Limavady

Nearest town
Limavady

Refreshments
Limavady

Public Toilets
Main Street, Limavady

Public Transport
Ulsterbus service 134 from Limavady to Coleraine travels along the A2 Seacoast Road stopping at Bellarena Primary School, Aghanloo (named in walk). If using public transport simply alter the start/finish point of the route.

Maps
Coleraine Discoverer Sheet 4
1:250,000 Northern Ireland Solid Geology

Nestled within the Binevenagh Area of Outstanding Natural Beauty, the Binevenagh walk offers wonderful views over Lough Foyle and the surrounding area, and provides an invigorating way to discover the breathtaking north-west coast of Northern Ireland.

Starting from the car park at Binevenagh Lake, facing towards the lake, take the path to the right hand side along the broad grassy track, following the waymarkers. The path soon turns to the right and follows the cliff edge. Please be careful not to get too close to the edge.

There are fantastic views over the mouth of the River Roe, Lough Foyle, Magilligan Point and Inishowen in Co. Donegal **(1)**. To the south lies the Sperrins, while to the north-east is the Causeway Coast, Rathlin Island and even the Western Isles of Scotland can be seen on a clear day.

As you continue along the cliff path, you will soon pass into the forest. Follow the track that leads off to the left down into the forest. You will leave the forest and see a track that leads off to the left. Follow this track downhill until it leads on to a broad path. Continue left and cross the stile that takes you into Binevenagh National Nature Reserve.

You will now be able to see the cliffs of Binevenagh clearly **(2)**. They are made up of individual flows of lava that cooled to form a dark igneous rock called basalt. The lava was erupted here some 60 million years ago and is part of a much larger area of basalt more commonly referred to as the Antim Plateau with Binevenagh at the north-western edge.

Keep walking with the forest to your right and go over another stile. Walk towards the edge of the forest and take a sharp right turn, still keeping the forest to your right. Walk downhill and go through a gate and turn left, walking diagonally across the field to another gate. At the gate turn right and follow the track (but don't go through the gate), and continue until you reach a stile at the end of the Nature Reserve. Go over the stile to the track and then turn left. Follow this track downhill ignoring all minor tracks leading off it. Continue on this track until you reach a T-junction, and turn right. Keep going on until reach another T-junction and turn right again.

Did you know?

Bishop's Road is named after the Earl Bishop of the nearby Downhill Estate. Born in 1730, it was the Earl Bishop that helped to first put the Giant's Causeway on the map. As a result of his pioneering work in vulcanology along the entire coastline he was made a fellow of the Royal Society.

Continue on this road and pass through the gate to join the main A2 road. Turn right and walk on the right hand side of the road, before carefully crossing the road and continuing on a footpath.

Much of the land here has been reclaimed from the sea and in some places it is only one or two metres above sea level. You are now on the flood plain of the River Roe that enters Lough Foyle just a few miles to the west.

Continue until you reach Bellarena Primary School where you turn right and walk up the Duncrun Road.

As you walk you will notice the irregular step-like features on Binevenagh **(3)**. These are landslips and are common around the plateau margins. At the foot of the cliffs are clays that formed in the Jurassic period, around 200 million years ago. Landslips occur here as hard blocks of basalt break off the steep plateau edge and sink into the soft Jurassic clays.

After about 1km a road to the right leads to Saint Aidan's Old Church and Holy Well **(4)**. The church dates from 1826, but the well is much older and would have more than likely pre-dated the coming of Christianity to Ireland. Many pagan sites would have been centred on natural water sources such as lakes, rivers and springs. The Holy Well found here is a natural spring, formed as water sinks below ground somewhere uphill, before flowing underground and finally reappearing at the surface here.

Return to the Duncrun Road and pass the Church of Ireland on the right hand side. Continue on and turn right up the Leighery Road.

Start

① ② ③ ④

Binevenagh Forest

BINEVENAGH

0   500   1000 metres

Crown Copyright 2017

Opposite: Traditional stone wall on the slopes of Binevenagh

Right: Binevenagh on the western edge of the Antrim Plateau with the River Roe in the background

Continue uphill until you reach a right turn signed to Binevenagh Lake, and follow the track back to the start point.

Barnes Gap

Barnes

GPS 54.758733, -7.144461 / Irish Grid H 55071 90430

Time: 3 hours
Distance: 11km (7 miles)
Grade: Leisurely
Type: Circular

Is it for me?
Suitable for adults and families with older children (8 years or older)

Start / Parking
The start point and car parking are at the picnic area at the foot of Barnes Gap signposted off the B47 Plumbridge to Draperstown Road

Nearest town
Gortin

Refreshments
Gortin

Public Toilets
Available at car park and Gortin

Public Transport
The Sperrins Rambler (Ulsterbus Service 403) stops at Cranagh from where it is 2km (1.2 miles) to the start of the walk

Maps
Sperrins Discoverer Sheet 13
Draperstown 1:50,000 Bedrock Geology Sheet 26

In the heart of the Sperrins Area of Outstanding Natural Beauty, the Barnes walk takes you through some of the most stunning glacial landscape in Northern Ireland steeped in both natural and cultural heritage.

Leave the picnic area and turn left and then take the second right, the Magherabrack Road, then walk up a steep hill to a farmyard. You will reach a junction at which you should turn right and continue walking up hill.

One of the first things you will see is the 'gap' known by many as Barnes Gap **(1)**. However, the name Barnes is actually an Irish word that simply means 'gap' so this is perhaps slightly confusing. The gap was cut by meltwater that drained under ice between the adjacent Owenkillew and Glenelly valleys throughout the ice age.

From the top of the hill at Barnes **(2)**, the view extends north over the high peaks of the Sperrin Mountains including Dart at 619m and Sawel at 678m, some of the highest in the range. Just after reaching the top of Barnes, a wide gravel track leads off to the left. Follow this track uphill.

As the path rises and bends away from Barnes, the view extends south to Mullaghcran and Gortin Forest Park. Bessy Bell mountain can be seen in the far distance to the south-west and gets its name from a Scottish folk song about two young girls called Bessy Bell and Mary Gray who died of the plague in the 17th Century. It is believed that Scottish immigrants on their way to America named these two hills after the girls in the song.

The path now skirts around the upper reaches of Gorticashel glen and the southern side of Mullaghbolig. As you continue to walk you will notice a large boulder in the adjacent field **(3)**. This boulder is a glacial erratic carried here by ice sheets during the last ice age. As you continue east, the hills of south Donegal come into view beyond Bessy Bell and the wide valley of Owenkillew becomes more obvious.

The path soon descends through another farmyard before meeting a tarred road. Turn right here and at the crossroads continue straight across. After about 200m another crossroads is reached so turn right and keep walking uphill along a gravel track.

Did you know?

The Owenkillew River contains the largest population of freshwater pearl mussels anywhere in Northern Ireland, and is one of only a few rivers that still maintain a population of this rare shellfish.

You will walk past an area of blanket bog on your left (4), a common habitat on the island of Ireland that is becoming increasingly threatened as they are cut for fuel. Blanket bogs have formed very recently, only 6,000 years ago when it was thought that the tree-felling activities of early settlers combined with a cooler and wetter climate encouraged their development.

After about 1km, the gravel lane comes to a T-junction with a narrow tarred road. Turn right and continue on until you reach the crossroads at the head of Barnes. Just before the crossroads you will see a rath, or an earthen ring fort that would have been built as a dwelling for an extended family and their livestock during early Christian times.

Turn left and walk downhill along the western side of Barnes. On the way back down the glen you will pass by some rock that has been exposed as a result of meltwater flow at the end of the last ice age. The rocks are mostly schist (5), a type of metamorphic rock that would have originally been mudstone, siltstone or sandstone. The mud would have been deposited on the floor of an ancient ocean that covered this area around 600 million years ago. The ocean eventually disappeared as continents on either side of it moved closer together and eventually collided with each other around 465 million years ago. The collision produced huge amounts of heat and pressure transforming, or metamorphosing the existing rocks into schist and raising them up to become part of an extensive mountain chain similar in size to the Himalayas. At that time, the mountain chain would have included the areas that we now know as the Donegal Highlands, the Scottish Highlands, Norway and eastern Northern America. The peaceful rounded

Opposite: Sawel Mountain

Right: Typical landscape along the Glenelly Valley

hills that we see today are the mere eroded roots of this former mountain range.

Return on the road for a further 1km until you reach the car park at the foot of Barnes.

Take a dander over the Sperrins.
Sense the myths hidden in bedrock
hear the echoes of the past reclaimed.

From 'The Sperrin Mountains' by Aine MacAodha

Lough Fea

Lough Fea

GPS 54.730419, -6.826715 / Irish Grid H 75577 87574

Time: 1 to 2 hours
Distance: 4km (3 miles)
Grade: Easy
Type: Circular

Is it for me?
Suitable for adults, families with older and younger children and dog walkers

Start / Parking
Car parking at Lough Fea on the B162 Cookstown to Draperstown Road

Nearest town
Cookstown/Draperstown

Refreshments
Cookstown/Draperstown

Public Toilets
Lough Fea Car Park

Maps
Sperrins Discoverer Sheet 13
1:250,000 Northern Ireland Solid Geology

Other Information
There is a children's play ground at the start of the walk

Set amidst wild mountain scenery, the Lough Fea walk encircles one of the many lakes found in the Sperrin Area of Outstanding Natural Beauty. The breathtaking scenery and the tranquil waters of Lough Fea makes this an idyllic location for a relaxing stroll.

The walk starts from the main car park at Lough Fea. Walk to the lake shore and turn right and approach the walk in an anti-clockwise direction.

Lough Fea is a spectacular example of a kettle lake and is just one of the many glacial landforms in the area that formed in the last ice age which ended a mere 13,000 years ago. Kettle lakes form as great chunks of ice break off retreating glaciers. Sand and gravel released from the melting glacier surrounds and covers the chunk of ice. As the ice continues to melt depressions form in the landscape which become filled with water.

As you continue round the lake there are great views of the surrounding hills and mountains (**1**). North of the lake the main Sperrins ridge is part of a much more extensive mountain range referred to as the Caledonides. The rocks of the Sperrins were laid down as sediments in an ocean called Iapetus but have since been subject to intense heat and pressure (metamorphism) that changed them into schists. This change occurred around 465 million years ago. Flat lying ground to the west of Lough Fea is underlain by volcanic rocks that formed on the margins of the Iapetus Ocean some 480-465 million years ago. It was the collision of these volcanic rocks and ocean crust with the rocks of the Sperrins that caused the mountain range to form.

Walking round the shores of the lake you will appreciate why this region is part of the Sperrin Area of Outstanding Natural Beauty. Aside from its rugged beauty and calming waters, Lough Fea is a haven for birdwatchers and you may see (or hear) merlin, hen harrier, buzzard, peregrine, long-eared owl, raven, red grouse, skylark and cuckoo along the way.

As the walk continues, you will follow the lake shore along the edge of a promontory that separates the two lobes of Lough Fea (**2**). Local legend suggests that this promontory and the matching one on the opposite shore represent the ghost of a man that drowned

Did you know?

The larger kettle hole of Lough Fea is the largest of its kind in Northern Ireland with an area of 180 acres. However, much larger ones exist in other parts of the world such as the largest in North America, the Puslinch Lake in Canada with an area of 400 acres.

here many years ago and the feature is known locally as Charlie's Ghost. In fact there are two kettle lakes at Lough Fea, a much larger one that you walk round for the majority of the first part of the walk and then in the south-east corner a much smaller one. The promontories are actually the remnants of a strip of sand and gravel that separated two kettle lakes. Through time this ridge of material eroded away and the two joined.

The landscapes of the Sperrins are a source of many natural resources. You will pass the Lough Fea Water Treatment Works (3), used to treat water from Lough Fea before it is pumped to Draperstown and the surrounding area. As you return to the start the walk you will also see a sand and gravel pit, on the opposite side of the main road. The sand and gravel was deposited at the end of the last ice age as glaciers melted leaving material behind.

The area around Lough Fea provides us with detailed information on how the glaciers melted, simply by studying the shape of the landscape and the types of material deposited. It also provides the construction industry with a valuable supply of sand and gravel (4), necessary for a number of processes including in the manufacture of concrete.

The walk carries on the footpath alongside the main road. If you are walking with small children, please take extra care at this point as the road can be busy. Continue until you return to the start point.

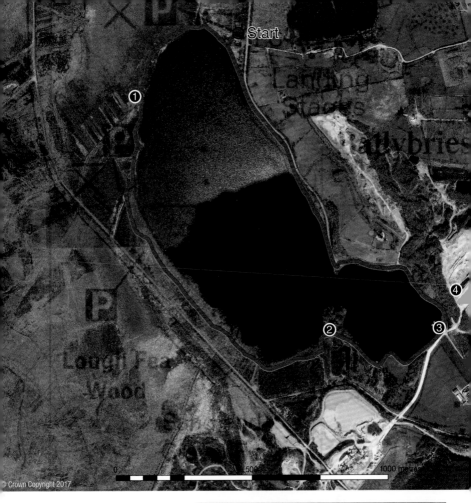

Start

① ② ③ ④

Landing Stages

Ballybries

Lough Fea Wood

P

P

0   500   1000 metres

© Crown Copyright 2017

Opposite: A view across the Sperrin Mountains that once made up a vast mountain chain called the Caledonides

Right: The vibrant purple heather along the shores of Lough Fea adds colour to a seasonally changing landscape

Fardross Forest

Fardross

GPS 54.385256, -7.201023 / Irish Grid H 51903 48818

Time: 2–3 hours
Distance: 7km (4.5 miles)
Grade: Easy
Type: Circular

Is it for me?
Suitable for adults, families with older children (8 years or older) and dog walkers

Start / Parking
The start point and car parking are at the entrance to Fardross Forest. This is signposted off the A4 (Belfast to Enniskillen) Road between Clogher and Fivemiletown.

Nearest town
Clogher

Refreshments
Clogher

Public Toilets
Signposted from Main Street, Clogher

Maps
Enniskillen Discoverer Sheet 18
1:250,000 Northern Ireland Solid Geology

The Fardross Forest Walk passes through parts of the old Fardross Estate and on to the uplands around the Clogher Valley. From gently gurgling streams to wild boglands, it is easy to see why the famous 19th Century writer William Carleton used his native area as inspiration.

Follow the waymarked River Walk, crossing the stream before turning right and continuing along the bank of the river. If water levels allow, cross the river when you reach the first set of stepping stones.

Upstream of the stepping stones, rocks are exposed in the river bank although partially obscured by vegetation **(1)**. The rocks comprise mudstones, siltstones and limestones and form thin layers, or beds, giving the exposure a striped appearance. If you look carefully enough, you will see that some of the layers contain fossil corals and sea-shells (known as brachiopods). Together these rocks make up a package known as a formation, meaning that they formed under similar environmental conditions. In this case the formation was deposited in a shallow tropical sea. The rocks exposed in the streambed either side of the stepping stones are examples of two different rock formations. Downstream the rocks are predominantly sandstones that were deposited in an ancient river delta.

As you walk beside the stream you pass through several rock formations that were laid down some 345–340 million years ago. The succession here tells us a story of changing sea level from a relatively deep to a shallow sea.

At the second set of stepping stones return across the river, ignoring the River Walk waymarkers and continue straight to the road. Turn right and cross the stream, then at the crossroads continue straight uphill eventually reaching open bogland. As you look back, views unfold across the Clogher Valley **(2)**. To the south is Slieve Beagh, while to the northeast the tower of Blackenridges Folly can be seen.

Keep following the road as it bends to the right and then back downhill. This section of the walk is part of the Carleton Trail, named after William Carleton, a famous writer in the early 19th

Did you know?

The fracture (or fault) in Slatmore Quarry is a branch of the much larger Clogher Valley fault. The location of this large fault has helped to control the formation of the valley, providing a line of weakness that was exploited by glaciers during the last ice age, and again by man as the route of the Clogher Valley railway up until the 1950s.

century who was born and raised in the Clogher Valley and took inspiration for much of his work from the surrounding landscapes.

Continue downhill, ignoring turnoffs until you reach a T-junction. At the junction turn right. Approximately 300m from the T-junction, you may catch a glimpse of Slatmore Quarry off to the right **(3)**.

The rock that is quarried here is limestone and is part of another geological formation, one that is commonly seen much further west. The reason that they are exposed here is that they were subject to intense earth movements, or faulting, which has moved them to their present position. Such movement caused the rocks to break up (or brecciate) into angular pieces, with the space in between now being infilled by the mineral calcite which gives the quarry face a criss-cross appearance. There are also slickensides (or parallel grooves) on the surface of the quarry which form as rock is forced past another rock along a fracture or fault. These rocks date back to about 345 million years ago so are older than those exposed in the forest.

Continue straight and rejoin the Carleton Trail at the next obvious junction and turn right back to the start.

Start

① ② ③

0   1000 metres

Opposite: The Clogher Valley

Right: Enjoying a forest walk

River Blackwater, Augher

Knockmany

GPS 54.410614, -7.172098 / Irish Grid H 53749 51662

Time: 5 hours
Distance: 13km (8 miles)
Grade: Leisurely
Type: Circular

Is it for me?
Suitable for adults, families with
older children (8 years and older)
and dog walkers

Start / Parking
On street parking in Clogher

Nearest town
Clogher

Refreshments
Clogher

Public Toilets
Signposted from Main Street,
Clogher

Public Transport
Goldline service 261 stops at
Clogher

Maps
Enniskillen Discoverer Sheet 18
1:250,000 Northern Ireland Solid
Geology

The beautiful towns and villages and the surrounding farmland
of the Clogher Valley are some of the most picturesque in
Northern Ireland. Rich in myths and legends, and loaded with a
wealth of natural and built heritage, their relaxed and tranquil
setting makes them a perfect place for a peaceful walk.

Depending on where you park, walk down hill and turn right just
after the fire station. Continue along this road passing through two
sets of crossroads. As you travel, you will notice a rath or ring-fort
on top of the small hill to the right **(1)**. This well-preserved example
dates back to early Christian times when such structures housed
an extended family and their livestock.

After the second crossroads, go on to the Forth Chapel or St.
Macartan's church **(2)**. St. Macartan was one of St. Patrick's
followers and first established a church in Clogher in the 5th
century. This church was the setting for 'Midnight Mass' a story
by the Irish writer and novelist William Carleton, who came from
Clogher.

Go back to the crossroads and turn right, continuing on until you
reach the village of Augher. Turn left at the T-junction and after
walking a short distance turn right at the roundabout in the village.
Walk for a few minutes before turning left off the road to walk along
the banks of the River Blackwater.

On the opposite bank of the river there are exposed sands and
gravels **(3)**. Ice sheets would have slowly crept down the entire
Clogher Valley during the last ice age and as they moved, they
would have gathered all sorts of debris including sand, gravel and
boulders. Such deposits would have simply been dumped on the
landscape as the huge ice sheets melted at the end of the last ice
age, around 13,000 years ago.

After the short walk along the river, take a right turn and follow
the signs for the Carleton Trail. The trail takes you off to the left
into Knockmany Wood, where there is a small car park and an
information panel. Keep on the trail and as you walk you will see
higher ground to the right while the lower ground of the Clogher
Valley is to the left. The higher ground is formed of harder rock that
is much more resistant to erosion than the rocks that underlie the
Clogher Valley. Movement along a fault or fracture in the Earth's

Did you know?

The famous 19th century novelist William Carleton was born in Clogher in 1794. His most well-known book Traits and Stories of the Irish Peasantry, tells of his experiences growing up in the rural landscapes of the Clogher Valley.

crust has brought these two different sets of rocks together. Although there has been no movement on the fault for millions of years, the surface expression still has an effect on the topography today.

Turn right at the fork in the track and go straight across the crossroads onto a less obvious track. Follow this uphill for about 30 minutes and then take the right hand path, following the signed track to the summit and cairn of Knockmany.

As you progress uphill, the forest thins and eventually gives way to grassy heath. On the left hand side of the track, orange-red rocks **(4)** are exposed. These rocks were formed in the Devonian period, around 380 million years ago and are some of the oldest rocks in the Clogher Valley. The rock is called conglomerate and is made up of rounded cobbles held together by sand. These rocks were deposited in rivers that flowed from a long-disappeared mountainous area to the north.

At the summit of Knockmany is Anya's Tomb **(5)**. This passage tomb dates back to Neolithic times and has three engraved stone slabs that are believed to be linked to Newgrange in Co. Meath. The name Anya is thought to be a reference to the legend of a 2nd century Queen called Aine who is believed to have been buried here.

Continue on the path down to a T-junction and turn left. Go through the gate and turn left at the road before following it around a left corner. As you descend, you will pass Lumford's Glen on your right hand side, obvious because of the trees that line the banks of the river that flows there **(6)**. Lumford's Glen is a great example of

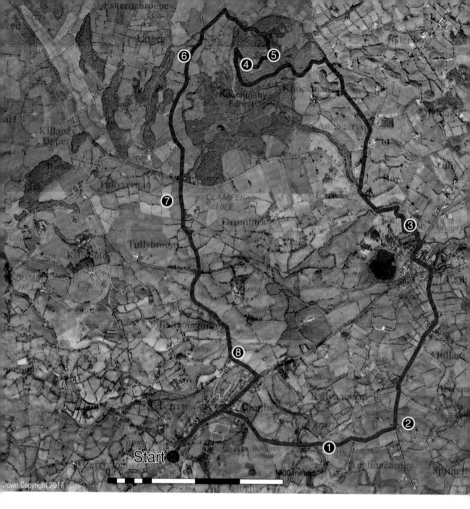

Opposite: The childhood home of the 19th century novelist William Carleton

native woodland and contains some very old oak and beech trees. However, the glen itself is better known for its connection to the giant Finn McCool who is said to have unearthed a spring here, and the resulting river now flows through the glen. During the summer the waterfall is often subdued but after heavy rainfall it is spectacular.

As you walk downhill you will see numerous small rounded hills known as drumlins **(7)**. The drumlins formed as ice sheets moved through the valley during the last ice age sculpting any loose material beneath them into the shapes that you now see.

Just before you return to Clogher, you will cross over Ballymagowan Bridge over the River Blackwater. Just next to the bridge is Bully's Acre, the cemetery for the nearby Clogher Union Workhouse **(8)**. Continue on this road and return to the Clogher, turning right to return to where you started.

Glossary

ammonite
An extinct group of marine animals, typically with a tightly coiled shell and often ornamented with ribs.

basalt
A volcanic igneous rock formed by the rapid cooling of lava.

bed
A layer of sedimentary rock.

belemnite
An extinct group of squid-like marine animals with a hard internal skeleton.

bivalve
An aquatic mollusc characterised by two identical shells that completely enclose the animal. Oysters, cockles and mussels are living examples.

blanket bog
An area of peatland that forms over large expanses of undulating ground.

calcium oxide
A chemical compound produced by the thermal decomposition of limestone (see quicklime).

Carboniferous
The geological time period lasting from 359Ma to 299Ma.

cave
A natural cavity or system of chambers beneath the surface of the Earth.

chalk
A white form of limestone composed primarily of coccoliths.

chert
A dense, extremely hard, microcrystalline sedimentary rock.

coal
A combustible black sedimentary rock formed by the carbonization of fossil plant material.

coccolith
The name given to individual plates of calcium carbonate formed by a type of algae known as coccolithophore.

conglomerate
A sedimentary rock consisting of individual rounded pebbles and / or cobbles held together by a finer matrix such as sand or silt.

crag and tail
A crag is a rocky hill, generally isolated from other high ground. Crags are formed when an ice sheet passes over an area that contains a particularly resistant rock formation. The force of the glacier erodes the surrounding

softer material, leaving the rocky block protruding from the surrounding terrain. Frequently the crag serves as a partial shelter to softer material in the wake of the glacier, which remains as a gradual fan or ridge forming a tapered ramp (called the tail) up the leeward side of the crag.

Cretaceous
The geological time period lasting from 145Ma to 66Ma.

crinoid
A marine animal belonging to the echinoderm family (such as star fish and sea urchins).

crust
The outermost layer of the Earth.

delta
The area where a river enters the sea (or other body of water) dividing itself into several arms and often forming an extensive wetland.

Devonian
The geological time period lasting from 419Ma to 359Ma.

dolerite
A form of intrusive igneous rock.

drumlin
An elongated elliptical hill formed by action of ice sheets.

dyke
A vertical sheet of intrusive igneous rock that cuts across layers of the host rock.

fault
A fracture in Earth materials along which movement has occurred.

Unesco Global Geopark
A Unesco designated territory with internationally important geological heritage and a sustainable tourism strategy.

glacial erratic
A glacially-transported boulder.

glacier
A body of dense ice exceeding 0.1km^2 and constantly moving under its own gravity.

granite
A common type of intrusive igneous rock.

granophyre
A type of intrusive igneous rock formed at shallow depths.

greywacke
A type of sandstone composed of angular grains set in a compact, clay-like matrix.

Iapetus Ocean
An ocean that existed between 420 and 600 million years ago.

ice age
A period of long-term reduction in global temperatures resulting in the expansion of continental and polar ice sheets.

ice sheet
A mass of ice that covers surrounding terrain and is greater than 50,000km^2.

igneous
A rock that has solidified from molten rock material which was generated from within the Earth.

iron ore
Rocks and minerals from which metallic iron is extracted.

Jurassic
The geological time period lasting from 201Ma to 145Ma.

kettle lake
A shallow sediment filled body of water formed by melting glaciers.

landslip / landslide
The name given to a variety of ground movements including rockfalls, slope failure, and debris flow that can occur in coastal, offshore and onshore environments.

lava
Molten rock that issues from an opening in the Earth's surface or on the ocean floor.

lignite
A soft brown fuel with characteristics between coal and peat.

lime kiln
A structure used to produce quicklime.

limestone
A sedimentary rock composed almost entirely of calcium carbonate.

Ma
Millions of years.

magma
Molten rock material.

meltwater
The water released by the melting of snow or ice.

metamorphic
Rocks that are the result of partial or complete recrystallisation as a result of conditions of temperature and / or pressure significantly different to those at the Earth's surface.

mud crack
A feature found in sedimentary rocks that forms as a result of muddy sediments drying and contracting.

mudmound
A build up of lime-rich mud that lacks any frame-building organism such as corals.

mudstone
A fine-grained sedimentary
rock composed chiefly of mud.

onion-skin weathering
A type of chemical weathering
that creates rounded boulders.

Palaeogene
The geological time period
lasting from 66Ma to 23Ma.

quicklime
A name given to calcium oxide
obtained by roasting lime in a
limekiln.

ripple
Preserved small-scale ridges
and troughs formed by the flow
of wind or water over loose
sediment.

sandstone
A sedimentary rock composed
of sand-sized grains.

schist
A metamorphic rock with
mica flakes in a preferred
orientation.

sill
A horizontal intrusion of molten
rock (or magma) between
existing layers of sedimentary
rocks, or other horizontal rock
layering.

siltstone
A fine-grained sedimentary
rock composed chiefly of silt.

Silurian
The geological time period
lasting from 443Ma to 419Ma.

slickensides
A smoothly polished surface
produced by frictional
movements between rocks
along the two sides of a fault.

spring
A natural flow of water from
underground, occurring where
the water table intersects the
ground surface.

Triassic
The geological time period that
lasted from 252Ma to 201Ma.

vent
A point where magma or gases
escape from beneath the
Earth's surface.

volcanic plug
A landform created when
magma hardens within a vent
on a volcano.

Useful contacts

Geological Survey of
Northern Ireland
Dundonald House
Upper Newtownards Road
Belfast
BT4 3SB
Tel: +44 (0)28 9038 8462
email: gsni@economy-ni.gov.uk
bgs.ac.uk/gsni

Belfast Hills Partnership
Hannahstown Hill
Belfast
BT17 0XS
Tel: +44 (0)28 9060 3466
belfasthills.org

Causeway Coast and Glens
Heritage Trust
The Old Bank
27 Main Street
Armoy
Ballymoney
BT53 8SL
Tel: +44 (0)28 2075 2100
ccght.org

Colin Glen Forest Park
163 Stewartstown Road
Dunmurry
Belfast
BT17 0HW
Tel: +44 (0)28 9061 4115
colinglentrust.org

Marble Arch Caves Unesco
Global Geopark
43 Marlbank Road
Florencecourt
Co. Fermanagh
BT92 1EW
Tel: +44 (0)28 6634 8855
marblearchcavesgeopark.com

Mourne Heritage Trust
19 Causeway Road
Newcastle
Co Down
BT33 0DL
Tel: +44 (0)28 4372 4059
mournelive.com

Ring of Gullion AONB
Crossmaglen Community Centre,
O'Fiaich Square
Crossmaglen
BT35 9AA
Tel: +44 (0)28 3086 1949
ringofgullion.org

Sperrins Gateway Landscape Partnership
The Old Soup Kitchen
Back Road
20b High Street
Draperstown
BT45 7AA
Tel: +44 (0)28 7962 8750
sperrinsgateway.com

Strangford Lough and Lecale Partnership
No.1 The Square
Portaferry
County Down
BT22 1LW
Tel: +44 (0)28 4272 8886
strangfordlough.org

Visitor information

For comprehensive information on what to see and do, where to eat and stay and transport across Northern Ireland visit the official website of the Northern Ireland Tourist Board.
discovernorthernireland.com

Below is a list of some of the Visitor Information Centres found in Northern Ireland. Services include information on the local area, the whole of Northern Ireland, activities, attractions, where to eat and accommodation booking services.

Belfast

Belfast City
Visit Belfast (Belfast & NI)
8-9 Donegall Square North
BT1 5GJ
Tel: +44 (0)28 9024 6609

County Antrim

Ballycastle
Portnagree House Harbour &
Marina Visitor Centre
14 Bayview Road
BT54 6BT
Tel: +44 (0)28 2076 2024

Giant's Causeway
44 Causeway Road
Bushmills
BT57 8SU
Tel: +44 (0)28 2073 1855

Portrush (seasonal)
Dunluce Centre
Sandhill Drive
BT56 8BF
Tel: +44 (0)28 7082 3333

County Armagh

Armagh
40 English Street
BT61 7BA
Tel: +44 (0)28 3752 1800

County Down

Newcastle
10-14 Central Promenade
BT33 0AA
Tel: +44 (0)28 4372 2222

Newry
Bagenal's Castle
Castle Street
BT34 2DA
Tel: +44 (0)28 3031 3170

Portaferry (seasonal)
The Stables
Castle Street
BT22 1NZ
Tel: +44 (0)28 4272 9882

County Fermanagh

Enniskillen
Wellington Road
BT74 7EF
Tel: +44 (0)28 6632 3110

County Londonderry

Coleraine
25 Railway Road
BT52 1PE
Tel: +44 (0)28 7034 4723

Limavady
Roe Valley Arts Cultural Centre
24 Main Street
BT49 0FJ
Tel: +44 (0)28 7776 0650

Londonderry / Derry
44 Foyle Street
BT48 6AT
Tel: +44 (0)28 7126 7284
E: info@derryvisitor.com

County Tyrone

Cookstown
The Burnavon
Burn Road
BT80 8DN
Tel: +44 (0)28 8676 9949

Omagh
Strule Arts Centre
Townhall Square
BT78 1BL
Tel: +44 (0)28 8224 7831

Public Transport

For all information on public
transport in Northern Ireland
please visit Translink at
translink.co.uk or
Tel: +44 (0)28 9066 6630